Fables of the Ancients?

Fables of the Ancients?

Folklore in the *Qur'an*

Alan Dundes

ROWMAN & LITTLEFIELD PUBLISHERS, INC.
Lanham • Boulder • New York • Oxford

ROWMAN & LITTLEFIELD PUBLISHERS, INC.

Published in the United States of America
by Rowman & Littlefield Publishers, Inc.
A Member of the Rowman & Littlefield Publishing Group
4501 Forbes Boulevard, Suite 200, Lanham, Maryland 20706
www.rowmanlittlefield.com

PO Box 317, Oxford, OX2 9RU, UK

Copyright © 2003 by Rowman & Littlefield Publishers, Inc.

All rights reserved. No part of this publication may be reproduced, stored
in a retrieval system, or transmitted in any form or by any means, electronic,
mechanical, photocopying, recording, or otherwise, without the prior permission
of the publisher.

British Library Cataloguing in Publication Information Available

Library of Congress Cataloging-in-Publication Data

Dundes, Alan.
   Fables of the ancients? : folklore in the Qur'an / Alan Dundes.
     p. cm.
   Includes bibliographical references and index.
   ISBN 0-7425-2671-2 (cloth : alk. paper) — ISBN 0-7425-2672-0 (pbk. :
alk. paper)
   1. Koran stories. 2. Koran—Evidences, authority, etc. I. Title.
   BP130.58.D86 2003
   297.1'226—dc21
                            2002154519

Printed in the United States of America

♾™ The paper used in this publication meets the minimum requirements of
American National Standard for Information Sciences—Permanence of Paper
for Printed Library Materials, ANSI/NISO Z39.48-1992.

To my six grandchildren:
David, Michael, Zachary, Madeline, Carolyn, and Katherine,
with the hope that their world will enjoy increased peace through
greater tolerance and understanding of religious differences

Contents

Preface	ix
Acknowledgments	xiii
What Is the *Qur'an*?	1
Oral-Formulaic Theory	15
Oral Formulas in the *Qur'an*	23
Folktales in the *Qur'an*	54
Conclusion	64
Bibliography	73
Index	85
About the Author	89

Preface

In May 1840, Thomas Carlyle (1795–1881) gave a series of six lectures on different sorts of heroes. These lectures were published as a book the year following, with chapters entitled "The Hero as Divinity," "The Hero as Prophet," "The Hero as Poet," "The Hero as Priest," "The Hero as Man of Letters," and "The Hero as King." Each chapter featured one or two examples. The "Poet" chapter discussed Dante and Shakespeare, while the second lecture devoted to the hero as prophet had a single subject, namely, Muhammad. This latter lecture, according to Carlyle himself, was the "best" one he had ever delivered (Carlyle 1993:xxviii).

Carlyle clearly admired Muhammad and he had praise for the religion founded by Muhammad, although he did insist that Islam was "a kind of Christianity." In the context of a milieu that tended to regard Muhammad as an impostor, responsible for creating an unfortunate rival or enemy of Christianity, Carlyle's essay was most remarkable for his stated belief in the absolute sincerity of Muhammad (Watt 1955:247). But what is no doubt most memorable about Carlyle's essay—and most often quoted—is his insulting invective supposedly summarizing his reaction to reading the *Qur'an*. "We also can read the Koran. . . . I must say, it is as toilsome reading as I ever undertook. A wearisome confused jumble, crude, incondite; endless iterations, long-windedness, entanglement; most crude, incondite:—insupportable stupidity, in short! Nothing but a sense of duty could carry any European through the *Koran*" (Carlyle 1993:56).

Preface

After the publication of *Holy Writ as Oral Lit: The Bible as Folklore* in 1999, in which I sought to demonstrate how traces of original oral transmission could be clearly discerned in both the Old and New Testaments, I began to wonder about other sacred texts that had a possible debt to oral tradition. One of the texts that aroused my curiosity was the *Qur'an*. As I began my research, I was almost immediately overwhelmed by the volume of scholarship devoted to the subject. Not only were there dozens of translations of the *Qur'an*, of varying quality, and numerous biographies of Muhammad, but there were countless monographs and articles devoted to different aspects of Islam, that is, religious practices, legal customs, attitudes toward women, and so on. Undeterred, I proceeded to read the *Qur'an* with a folklorist's eye, using several of the standard methodological instruments found in the international folklore toolkit. I soon discovered that there seemed to be many "formulas" as well as several traditional stories, stories that were not simply retellings of narratives found in the Bible. To my knowledge, no folklorist has ever discussed the presence of both formulas and folktales in the *Qur'an*.

In order to verify my suspicion that this kind of folkloristic study had not been attempted hitherto, I began to check with trusted colleagues here in the United States and abroad. There were two basic responses. No, this type of investigation had not been carried out before, but also, there was a unanimous opinion expressed that I should under no circumstances attempt such a study. In fact, I was warned that it might even be dangerous for me to do so. I was told that such a study might be judged demeaning and considered as a form of disparagement of the *Qur'an*. This well-intentioned caution from specialists in Arabic folklore only piqued my interest further and, indeed, emboldened me to go ahead with my project.

In October 2001, I unexpectedly received an invitation from Professor Monia Hejaiej of the Institut Superieur des Langues de Tunis, organizer of the Second International Conference on Middle Eastern and North African Popular Culture, held at the Hammamet International Center, April 23–26, 2002, to give the keynote address at the conference. I was pleased to accept the invitation, in part because the occasion provided me with a perfect opportunity to present a preliminary version of this work, for which I remain most grateful. The incisive comments and criticisms offered by the participants, almost all of whom were specialists in Arabic language and literature, helped me clarify my thesis and its implications.

Finally, I should like to make a prediction that Western readers will no doubt find this essay to be rather bland. For them, the empirical data presented is likely to appear matter-of-fact and unexceptional. However, I would like to think that Islamic scholars possessing true expertise in the study of the *Qur'an* will find in this work a radical departure from the long history of conventional approaches to this sacred text. And I hope in any event that I, who am neither Islamophile nor Islamophobe, will have shown that the *Qur'an* is hardly "a wearisome confused jumble," as Carlyle contended so many years ago.

Acknowledgments

As a nonspecialist in Arabic literature or in *Qur'an*ic studies, I have had to rely upon the extensive literature devoted to the *Qur'an*. I shall not single out individual works, as I have sought to acknowledge my sources in the usual academic fashion, sources duly listed in the bibliography. The one exception is Hanna E. Kassis's *A Concordance of the Qur'an*, a magnum opus published by the University of California Press in 1983, whose 1,444 pages of detail, in effect, made it possible for me to carry out this research expeditiously.

I must also thank Jo Lynn Milardovich, Elissa Mondschein, Helen Ram, Charlotte Rubens, Maureen Davis, Teresa Moore, and the other outstanding members of the Interlibrary Loan section of Doe Memorial Library who were consistently able to locate copies of hard-to-find crucial monographs and articles, essential for my project. Their extraordinary sleuthing skills never cease to amaze me and I have appreciated their many efforts for more than three decades on my behalf.

I owe a special debt to my colleague James T. Monroe, professor of Arabic and comparative literature at the University of California, Berkeley, for his kindness in reading this essay. His encyclopedic knowledge of medieval Arabic language and literature helped me avoid making a number of mistakes. Any remaining errors of either fact or interpretation, however, are entirely my responsibility.

Finally, I wish to express once again my heartfelt gratitude to editor Dean Birkenkamp of Rowman & Littlefield, who has been a stalwart source of strength and encouragement in this as in many of my previous projects, the unconventional nature of which has not always made his editorial task an easy one. His unwavering support over the years—even in times of crisis—is something I shall always value.

Fables of the Ancients?
Folklore in the *Qur'an*

"In this *Qur'an*, We have set forth for mankind all manner of parables but man is the most contentious of creatures" (18:54).

WHAT IS THE *QUR'AN*?

*I*slam is one of the world's great religions. Like many of the great religions, Islam is based on a charter-book. As the Jews have their Torah and the Christians have their Bible, especially the New Testament, so the Muslims have the *Qur'an*. The *Qur'an* has received high praise from Muslim and non-Muslim alike. It has been called "the most beautiful of all works in the Arabic language, a book whose eloquence is itself the greatest miracle in Islam" (Nasr 1972:42) and "by far the finest work of Arabic prose in existence" (Jones 1994:ix).

The *Qur'an*—this is the spelling preferred by most Muslims rather than the English *Koran*—is believed to be the literal word of Allah or God as revealed to the Prophet Muhammad, ostensibly through the intermediation of the archangel Gabriel, the same Gabriel who explained visions to the prophet Daniel (Daniel 8:16, 9:21) and who informed Zacharias of the future birth of John the Baptist and also announced the birth of Jesus to the Virgin Mary (Luke 1:19, 26).

It is understood that Muhammad was "in no sense the author of the *Qur'an*. He simply received the *Qur'an* in the form of an oral deliverance from the Angel and transmitted it in the same form to his contemporaries" (Said 1975:56). "Neither does he [Muhammad] speak of his own will, This [the *Qur'an*] is naught but a revelation revealed to him" (53:3–4). "It is not for me [Muhammad] to change it of my own accord. I follow only what is revealed to me" (10:15; cf. 46:9). "This *Qur'an* has been revealed to me so that I may thereby warn you and all whom it may reach" (6:19). The "author," so to speak, of the *Qur'an* is Allah and "there is no credible evidence in the *Qur'an* to suggest that its authorship can be attributed to the Prophet" (Saeed 1999:110). Nothing infuriates a true believer in Islam more than the contention that it was Muhammad who composed the *Qur'an*, making it a human creation or composition rather than a holy transcendent sacred document. As Muhammad was said to be illiterate, he had to commit the *Qur'an* to memory so that he could transmit it accurately to his followers. The allusion to illiteracy is found in the twenty-ninth surah or chapter entitled "The Spider," when Allah addresses Muhammad: "Never have you read a book before this, nor have you ever transcribed one with your right hand" (29:48). Muhammad's enemies claimed that he had arranged to have stories of the ancients written down so that "they could be read out to him morning and evening" (26:6), another indication that he was unable to read and write. "It is not the words of a poet . . . nor the words of a soothsayer. . . . It is a revelation from the Lord of the Universe" (69:41–43). Whether or not Muhammad was actually illiterate is in dispute. One theory is that he only feigned illiteracy in order to emphasize the miraculous nature of the divine revelation and to remove any possible speculation that he had composed the *Qur'an* himself (Zwemer 1939:100–120), but the majority view is that Muhammad was illiterate because the *Qur'an* says he was (Rashid 1995). As one writer phrases it, for the believer, Muhammad was a blank page upon which was inscribed a pre-existing divine text (Benslama 1988:47).

If Muhammad were truly illiterate, unable to read and write, the very first word supposedly uttered by Allah to him via Gabriel seems somewhat paradoxical. It appears in surah 96, the surah said to be the first of the one hundred and fourteen transmitted to Muhammad (al Imam 1998:38), and the word was: "Read!" (or "Recite!") (96:1). An equally puzzling passage with respect to the illiteracy issue is found in one of the many accounts of the Day of Judgment, Resurrection Day, according to which, each believer saved is said to be given a book containing a record of his life. The saved soul is then given the command: "Read thy book" (17:12, cf. 17:71, 69:19), a command that in theory would prove difficult for anyone unable to read (Benslama 1988:64).

According to tradition, Muhammad did not receive the entire *Qur'an* at one time. Instead, the complete set of 114 chapters or "surahs," each consisting of a number of verses ranging from 3 to 286, was communicated by Allah in installments, piecemeal over a period of twenty-three years, essentially over the lifetime of the Prophet following the initial revelation, which occurred in Muhammad's fortieth year. "It is a *Qur'an* that We have divided into parts from time to time in order that you might recite it to men at intervals: We have revealed it by stages" (17:106). The surahs are not presented in the *Qur'an* in chronological or linear fashion. In other words, the sequence of surahs reflects neither the order in which they were revealed by Allah to Muhammad nor the evident chronology of the historical events described in the *Qur'an*. Rather, the order is determined by the length of the surahs, with the longer ones at the beginning and the shorter ones at the end. As already mentioned, the very first surah revealed to Muhammad in Mecca is positioned near the end of the *Qur'an*. It is surah 96 that begins "Read (or Recite) in the name of your Lord who created" (al Imam 1998:38; for a discussion of the surah as a unit of the *Qur'an*, see Mir 1993).

Muhammad was born circa 570 and reportedly the first portion of the *Qur'an* was revealed to him during Ramadan (2:185), the traditional month of fasting, around the year 610. Most of the *Qur'an* is presumed to have been revealed in Mecca but some portions were alleged to have been disclosed after Muhammad migrated to Medina in 622. (One of the first attempts to distinguish the Meccan surahs from those revealed in Medina was Theodor Nöldeke's *Geschichte des Qorans*, first published in 1860.) In any case, the intermittent communication continued over a period of some twenty-three years until his death in 632.

During Muhammad's life, his companions and wives recorded various portions of the *Qur'an* as recited by the Prophet. After his death, a concerted effort was made to collate these diverse records into an official canonical version. There is some consensus that this was successfully accomplished under the aegis of Caliph Uthman from 644 to 656. Nevertheless, there were conflicting and competing codices, not all of which were ever entirely quashed. According to one source, there are one hundred and twenty-three differences between the accepted canonical text of the *Qur'an* and the personal codices of Muhammad's companions (al Imam 1998:86). In 1972, a cache of *Qur'an* fragments, totaling more than 15,000 sheets, was discovered during the restoration of the Great Mosque of Sana'a in Yemen, several of these fragments dating back to the seventh and eighth centuries and revealing minor but interesting "deviations from the standard Koranic text" (Lester 1999:44). Some of the deviations have to do with different arrangements of the sequential order of the surahs (Puin 1996:111). According to one tradition, when Caliph Uthman noticed several "irregularities" or apparent outright "errors" in the copies of the *Qur'an* submitted to him, he is alleged to have said "Do not change them; the Arabs will change (or correct) them as they recite" (Burton 1988:181). Such a comment, even if apocryphal, would seem to anticipate folklorist Walter Anderson's so-called "Gesetz der Selbstrichtigung" or "Law of Self-Correction," according to which principle, oral tradition has the capacity to correct itself in the event that an individual link in the oral transmission process gave a faulty or incomplete rendering of a given item (Bødker 1965:124; Krohn 1971:123). The idea is that a narrator will hear a particular narrative more than one time, often from different sources, and that in the process any error or omission will be corrected. Yet, in the case of the *Qur'an*, the point is that even the most trivial or relatively inconsequential deviation presents a serious problem for those who believe in the sacrosanct existence of the *Qur'an* as an unchanging, immutable record of the word of God. In that sense, Muslim true believers share a notion analogous to the Christian doctrine of "inerrancy" (Dundes 1999:116), according to which, since the Bible is the word of God, it cannot possibly contain anything untrue or in error. Accordingly, the suggestion or claim that there are actual "linguistic errors" in the *Qur'an* (cf. Burton 1988; Dashti 1985:48–51) borders on blasphemy, even if such "errors" were simply attributed to faulty copyists (Bellamy 1973:273, n 41). Given the "official" account of the *Qur'an*'s origins, one can see that the partially divine *isnad* (chain of transmission) might well provide an opportunity for mistakes to inadvertently creep in. Allah communicates the text to Gabriel who communicates the text to Muhammad who communicates the text to his followers who communicate it to mankind (Wild 1993:258). Of course, if it were assumed that Muhammad were either the sole "human author" of the *Qur'an* or had somehow tampered editorially with it, perhaps unintentionally, that would be another way to avoid attributing any "mistakes" or "inaccuracies" to Allah (Saeed 1999:94), but as already noted, that supposition runs absolutely counter to basic Islamic doctrine. The *Qur'an* is very clear on this point: "There is no changing the words of Allah" (10:64) and "No man can change the words of Allah" (6:34, 115, 18:27). The absolute inviolable fixity of the content of the *Qur'an* is affirmed in no uncertain terms. "You shall find no change in the ways of Allah" (33:62, 35:43, 48:23). An extreme position stemming from a presumption of the "inerrancy" of the *Qur'an* is that if there appear to be grammatical errors in the *Qur'an*, then the rules of Arabic grammar obviously need to be changed. As one writer phrases it: "Our task is not to make the readings conform to Arabic grammar, but to take the whole of the *Qur'an* as it is and make Arabic grammar conform to the *Qur'an*" (Dashti 1985:50). Clearly, the *Qur'an* represents a quintessential *fons et origo*. A slightly more moderate Muslim view suggests "that even though the *Qur'an* is undoubtedly the Word of God, it is revealed in the language and locution of man, and its way of expression is exactly the same as that of a well-spoken Arab whose eloquence is unparalleled" (Baljon 1961:44). It goes without saying that this is definitely not the position taken by the more devout and partisan adherents of Islam.

6 Fables of the Ancients?

The history of the establishment of a definitive text of the *Qur'an* is a complex one and is not our concern in this essay. (For a sampling of the many discussions of this history, see Burton 1972, 1977; Watt 1970:40–56; al Imam 1998:23–62; Warraq 1998; and Motzki 2001; for a consideration of the degrees of accuracy of the transmission of the text and *hadith*, sayings attributed to Muhammad or his companions, commenting on the text, see Robson 1953; Donner 1998; and Motzki 2001.) Nor am I concerned with questions as to the degree of historicity of details in the life of Muhammad as extrapolated from the *Qur'an*, another subject of heated debate (Rodinson 1981; Rippin 2000; Warraq 2000). Similarly, I am not interested in superficial speculations about Muhammad's personality, pathological or otherwise, based on information contained in the *Qur'an*, even if supplemented by data from the *hadith* (Berkeley-Hill 1921; Berg 1966; Aslam 1968). Admittedly, his reported encounters and conversations with the archangel Gabriel as well as his mystical night journey (or a vision of such) in which he was magically teleported from Mecca to Jerusalem, accompanied by Gabriel (17:1), provide potential fodder for medical or psychological interpretation. One such theory holds that Muhammad's visions were induced by psychomotor seizures connected with an epileptic condition (Freemon 1976; cf. Sprenger 1889). This would tend to make the *Qur'an* essentially the result of an extended hallucination (Benslama 1988:59). One of the detractors quoted in the *Qur'an* itself refers to the *Qur'an* as "but a medley of dreams" (21:5, cf. 12:44).

There is also the matter of Muhammad's various marriages. It is tempting, for example, to see a connection between the loss of his widowed mother Amina at the tender age of six and his initial (Oedipal?) marriage to his employer Khadija, a wealthy widow fifteen years his senior, not to mention his subsequent marriage to his cousin Zaynab, the divorced wife of his adopted son Zayd, or his marriage to the seven-year-old Ayesha who eventually became one of his favorite wives. The equation of wife and mother is signaled by the traditional divorce verbal formula allegedly uttered by a man to his spouse: "Thy back to me as the back of my mother." It may be relevant that the Arabic word for "back" in this formula, namely "zahr," is reportedly a euphemism (Mir 1989:228). In any case, the Oedipal implications of the formula are implicitly recognized in the *Qur'an*: "Allah does not regard the wives whom you divorce as your mothers, nor your adopted sons as your own sons" (33:3). The latter portion of the passage similarly seeks to circumvent the near incestuous aspects of Muhammad's marriage to Zaynab. Another implicit interdiction against symbolic incest is the injunction forbidding a man to marry his father's widow: "You shall not marry the women whom your fathers married" (4:22), which is followed immediately by "Forbidden to you are your mothers, your daughters, your sisters" (4:23). Still, if the *Qur'an* is really the word of God, and if Muhammad's role is merely that of a more or less passive instrument of transmission whereby he adds or subtracts nothing from the sacred revelation, then it would be foolhardy to attempt a psychohistorical analysis of Muhammad from the *Qur'an*. The *Qur'an* as text could provide only a means of analyzing the personality of its true author, that is, Gabriel or Allah Himself, not Muhammad.

One obvious problem in arriving at a clear notion of a final "correct" text of the *Qur'an* is the fact that Muhammad evidently forgot portions of it or uttered contradictory passages. The *Qur'an* itself recognizes this difficulty: "We shall make you recite Our revelations, so that you shall forget none of them except as Allah pleases" (87:6). Presumably it was the will of Allah that certain passages were forgotten or negated. "If we abrogate a verse or cause it to be forgotten, We will replace it by a better one or one similar" (2:106). "Allah abrogates and confirms what He pleases" (13:39). "When we change one verse for another (Allah knows best what He reveals)" (16:101). The overt and explicit acknowledgment in the *Qur'an* itself of the existence of abrogation would appear to argue against the notion of the perfect concinnity of the *Qur'an*. One problem, however, with respect to the issue of perfection is that if Allah were truly without fault, why would He have made a statement in the first place that later had to be negated or nullified (Dashti 1985:156)?

Abrogation did not succeed in removing all of the apparent contradictions in the *Qur'an*. One illustrative example should suffice. True believers in Islam are in theory not supposed to imbibe wine. The *Qur'an* is very clear and specific about this taboo. "Oh believers, wine and games of chance, idols and divining arrows are all machinations of Satan. Avoid them so that you may prosper. Satan seeks to create enmity and hatred among you by means of wine and gambling, and to keep you from the remembrance of Allah and from your prayers. Will you therefore not abstain from them?" (5:90–91, cf. 2:219). If wine is off limits, then it is surely surprising to find that one of the four rivers that flow in paradise contains "delectable" wine. "The picture of paradise as promised to the pious includes rivers of unpolluted water, rivers of forever fresh milk, rivers of wine delectable to drinkers, and rivers of clarified honey" (47:15). In the *Qur'an*, we are also told that in the afterlife, "They will be offering and receiving cups of wine" (52:23) (Mir 1989:344). So on the one hand, wine is the work of the devil, and on the other hand, wine is part of the heavenly bounty provided by Allah, although elsewhere the celestial "white" wine (Mir 1989:223) is said to be not intoxicating (37:47, 52:23, 56:19). If it were intoxicating, it might induce "idle talk," which is not permitted in heaven (19:62, 52:23, 56:25, 78:35).

According to several scholars, the disparity between wine being forbidden on earth but permitted in paradise is part of a larger contrastive paradigm. The paradigm consists of a "triad of sins" (Monroe 1997:118) consisting of fornication, pederasty, and wine drinking, all of which are interdicted on earth because, at least in the case of the first two sins, they are not designed to fulfill the obligation to propagate the species (Stetkevych 1997: 227). In paradise, there is no need of conjugal sexual reproduction so that there it is perfectly all right for males to have access to both nubile virgins, the so-called *houris,* and pubescent boy cupbearers—"They shall be attended by boys graced with eternal youth" (76:19).

The "contradictions" issue is dealt with reflexively in the *Qur'an* itself. Since the *Qur'an* is the word of Allah, there simply cannot be contradictions. "If it were from other than Allah, they would surely have found in it many contradictions" (4:82). The reasoning is seemingly analogous to that employed to rebut the charge that there are grammatical "errors" in the *Qur'an*, mentioned above.

Because the words of the *Qur'an* are deemed to be of godly origin, specifically communicated to Muhammad by the archangel Gabriel in Arabic, translations of the *Qur'an* in other languages are deemed to be somewhat spurious and not considered reliable for purposes of analysis. There are at least two meanings of the doctrine of the untranslatability of the *Qur'an*. One is that it would be a sin to translate it and the second is that any translation of the *Qur'an* from Arabic into any other language would fail to faithfully represent the "original" (Rahbar 1963:60), if for no other reason than the fact that there are metaphors (Sabbagh 1943) and idioms in the *Qur'an* that virtually defy facile translation (Mir 1989:10–13). (In consulting eight different English translations of the *Qur'an*, I found great disparities in the rendering of the "same" passage.) There are many statements referring to one or the other of these views. "It is an unavoidable truth that it is not lawful to proceed to make a translation of the Holy *Qur'an*" (Shakir 1926:165). The twelfth surah, entitled "Joseph," of the *Qur'an* itself begins, "These are the verses of the Glorious Book. We have revealed the *Qur'an* in the Arabic tongue so that you may grow in understanding" (12:2). There are many reiterations in the *Qur'an* of its being in Arabic: "Thus as a code of judgments in the Arabic tongue have we sent down the *Qur'an*" (13:37). "We have sent it down: a *Qur'an* in the Arabic tongue" (20:113) and "We have revealed to you an Arabic *Qur'an*" (42:7, cf. 26:195, 39:28, 41:3, 46:12). Similarly, in the forty-third surah, we are told, "We have revealed the *Qur'an* in the Arabic tongue that you may understand its meaning. It is a transcript of the eternal book in Our keeping, sublime, and full of wisdom" (43:3).

There are numerous dialects of Arabic and there is some debate as to why one particular dialect of Arabic was evidently selected by Allah as the language of choice for the *Qur'an* (al Imam 1998:91–111). Whether every single word of the *Qur'an* is to be adjudged pure Arabic is open to question, as scholars have documented the existence of loan words from other languages in the text (Jeffery 1938). Supposedly the apparent infelicities and contradictions enumerated by Orientalists disappear if the *Qur'an* is read in the original Arabic. (For a discussion of the various English translations of the *Qur'an*—there are more than forty according to Robinson [1996:291]—and some of the mistaken interpretations said to have resulted therefrom, see Khalifa 1983:64–79). The long-standing mistrust of translations of the *Qur'an* is not an issue easily understood by Euro-Americans who for the most part are perfectly comfortable reading their Bible in English, French, German, and so on, even though they may be intellectually well aware of the fact that when God spoke to Moses or when Jesus spoke to his disciples, the language used was none of these but presumably Hebrew and Aramaic. In other words, most practicing Christians see no problem in reading their holy book in their own native language. They might feel differently, though, if they believed that their sacred scripture had been originally revealed *in* that native language.

The exclusivity of the Arabic text of the *Qur'an* has caused difficulties even within Islam. According to one authority, only about 25 percent of the world's more than one billion Muslims are native speakers of Arabic (Cook 2000:7, 26). This means that they are outnumbered by non-Arabic-speaking Muslims such as those who speak Farsi, Turkish, and Indonesian, among other languages. There are roughly forty-five countries whose population is more than half Muslim (al Faruqi 1987a:2). Many of these Muslims, not knowing Arabic, obviously have some interest in reading the *Qur'an* in their own native language, even if as children they learned to recite the *Qur'an* by rote in Arabic. Yet the problem of translation is just one of the problems facing scholars interested in studying the *Qur'an*.

Since the words of the *Qur'an* consist of Allah's actual speech, it is thought to be sacrilegious to apply human literary or philological techniques to such sacred language. In fact, it is politically incorrect, not to say dangerous, for Arab scholars to do so. In Muslim universities, academics are for the most part reluctant, to say the least, to treat the text of the *Qur'an* as they would any literary document, secular or sacred. To do so would run the risk of being accused of blasphemy or worse. This is not idle speculation on my part. The situation of former University of Cairo Professor of Arabic Language and Literature Nasr Hamid Abu Zayd is a case in point. After he published his controversial 1992 book *Naqd al-Khitab al-Dini* involving a critique of religious discourse in which he proposed studying and reinterpreting religious texts including the *Qur'an* in terms of their original historical and social context, he was accused of having defamed Islam. One of his premises was that once the *Qur'an* was revealed to Muhammad, it entered the realm of human history and could therefore be studied as such (Zeid 1999:28; cf. Wild 1993). The crux of the resulting dispute arises from Islamic fundamentalists claiming it was not permissible to treat a "divine" text as though it were a human, manmade, cultural product. According to this reasoning, it is wrong, if not tantamount to a sacrilegious act, to subject a divine text to human textual criteria (Zeid 1999:32). In this context, the application of any standard theory or method whatsoever to the *Qur'an* would be regarded negatively by Muslims as an unwarranted "imposition from outside the text" and as an unjustified, unwelcome "humanizing intrusion on the divine text" (al Faruqi 1987a:9). For if one were somehow permitted to apply scientific principles and reason to the *Qur'an*, it might be possible to demythologize it by eliminating any false or mythical elements (Hirschkind 1995:38, 40).

The "Court of Cassation" was evidently particularly alarmed by Abu Zayd's apparent denial of the existence of genies or "jinn," which are repeatedly referred to in the *Qur'an* (Cook 2000:47). For instance, Allah Himself acknowledges that he invented jinn for a specific purpose: "I have created jinn and mankind only that they might serve Me" (51:56). And He also vows, "I will fill Hell with jinn and men together" (11:119, 32:13). The power of the jinn was limited. Even "if all men and all the jinn joined forces to produce a book like the *Qur'an*, they could never succeed in doing so no matter how much they helped one another" (17:88). This certainly emphasizes both the divine origin of the *Qur'an* and its inimitable nature, but it is also yet another reference to the very existence of jinn. The jinn were reportedly created by Allah "from smokeless fire" (55:15, cf. 15:27). Furthermore, one of the surahs, namely surah 72, is even entitled "The Jinns" and, finally, jinn are mentioned in the very last line of the last surah of the *Qur'an* (114:6). Zayd's position is that jinns and demons might be mental representations belonging to a certain stage of the evolution of human consciousness (Zeid 1999:75), an idea that had been proposed earlier by other scholars (Rahman 1980:123). It is interesting in this connection that some of the English translations of the *Qur'an* omit any references to jinn (Robinson 1996:231). In any event, the court's verdict of 4 August 1996 declared Professor Abu Zayd to be an apostate or heretic. According to one authority who discussed this case, "The orthodox Muslim view maintains that a person who abandons Islam commits apostasy and must be put to death" (Sfeir 1998:409). In this instance, the death penalty was not imposed. Nevertheless, not only was Abu Zayd subsequently denied tenure at his university but since Islamic rules do not permit a Muslim woman to be married to an apostate from Islam, he was ordered to separate from his wife who was also an academic. It was earlier, in June 1995, that an Egyptian government court had dissolved Abu Zayd's marriage to Dr. Ibtihal Younis without the couple's consent (Wild 1996:xi). Fortunately, the couple refused to be divorced and found refuge at the University of Leiden in Holland. In the present context, it is of interest that although Abu Zayd specifically criticized misguided critics who, through what he termed "gross ignorance," sought to relegate the *Qur'an* to the status of "folklore," he himself was publicly accused of doing precisely that (Zeid 1999:44, 52).

It should be noted that the case of Abu Zayd is by no means unique. Earlier in Egypt, in 1926, another academic, Taha Husain, published *Fi'sh–Shi-r al-Jahili*, "in which he questioned the historical veracity of the *Qur'an*. Charged with blasphemy, he was forced to withdraw his book, and lost his university post" (Warraq 1995:6, 2000:23). Another celebrated instance occurred in 1947 when a young professor at the University of Fouad in Cairo named Mohammad Ahmad Khalafallah submitted his doctoral dissertation, which consisted of a literary analysis of the *Qur'an*. Part of his thesis involved dismissing criticisms of the *Qur'an* that had to do with apparent historical inaccuracies. He argued that such minor issues were trivial and of little import. From a literary perspective, the *Qur'an*, he suggested, should be seen as a divine document seeking to put man on the right spiritual path and thus poetic license was permitted, which included taking liberties with the historical record. Accordingly, Old and New Testament accounts could be retold and secular legends could be utilized in a manner reflecting the specifics of Muhammad's situation vis-à-vis his detractors and critics in order to get the spiritual message across (Jomier 1954). Khalafallah's dissertation was rejected by his committee on the grounds that it was blasphemous. His apparent acceptance of the lack of historicity of any portion of the *Qur'an*, no matter how minute such a detail might be, was considered to be sacrilegious. The local press got wind of the matter and it caused quite a public furor. Khalafallah then revised his dissertation, taking out some of the disputed sections. This version was also rejected (although it was published in 1951). He finally received his degree much later, after presenting an entirely different thesis, written on a totally secular subject (Jomier 1954:48).

Non-Muslims have also refrained from analyzing the *Qur'an* using the techniques of so-called "higher criticism," fearing that such research would be summarily dismissed as nothing more than the improper and misguided efforts of orientalists. This is why the majority of western Arabists, having no wish to unnecessarily offend their Muslim colleagues, have elected to steer clear of any analysis of the *Qur'an* that might be judged demeaning or insulting (Warraq 1995:24). It is not just in the Arab world that it can prove to be perilous to one's career to analyze the *Qur'an* in a nonauthorized fashion. The German Islamicist Günter Lüling learned this when he submitted his doctoral dissertation at the University of Erlangen in 1970, which suggested that the *Qur'an* contained evidence of traces of poetic strophic texts, a view not in accord with orthodox Islamic tradition. By 1972, he was officially dismissed from his university, and a six-year legal struggle did not succeed in reversing the university's action (Lüling 1996:95–99).

As a consequence of the long-standing resistance to applying standard "literary" and other conventional modes of analysis to the *Qur'an*, there has been understandably relatively little folkloristic analysis of the *Qur'an*. The present essay should in that light be regarded as a modest attempt to look at the *Qur'an* from a folkloristic perspective. Certainly no disrespect toward this remarkable document is intended. Quite the contrary. As one of the most important religious documents ever to be created, the *Qur'an* deserves nothing less than our sincerest efforts to illuminate its very nature.

The *Qur'an* is frequently referred to as a "book" and in fact is often thought to represent an exact replica of an actual holy book existing in pristine form as a "preserved tablet" in heaven. "Surely this is a glorious *Qur'an* inscribed on an imperishable tablet" (85:22). "Should I [Muhammad] seek a judge other than Allah when it is He who has revealed the Book for you with all its precepts?" (6:115). "It is a revelation from Him who has created the earth and the lofty heavens" (20:4). "This is a glorious *Qur'an*, safeguarded in a book which none may touch except the purified; a revelation from the Lord of the Universe" (56:78–79). "We have revealed the Book which manifests the truth about all things" (16:89). From a psychological perspective, it is of interest that the "original" of the *Qur'an*, located in heaven, is referred to literally as the "**Mother**" of the book (3:7, 13:39, 43:4), although it is not always translated as such in English versions of the *Qur'an*. This original "mother" is inaccessible to humankind (cf. Benslama 1988:87), including Muhammad, and belongs entirely to Allah, a masculine, paternal deity, a configuration with possible Oedipal implications. Freud in his final book, *Moses and Monotheism*, claimed that "The regaining of the one great primeval Father produced in the Arabs an extraordinary advance in self-confidence which led them to great worldly successes," adding that "Allah proved himself to be much more grateful to his chosen people than Jahve had in his time" (1955:118). However, our concern here is not with the "original" book and its possible maternal aspects but rather with its connection with the process of oral transmission.

Just as the *Qur'an* was recited orally by Gabriel to Muhammad who in turn recited it orally to his followers, so to this day the *Qur'an* is supposed to be recited orally to the faithful who are encouraged to recite it orally themselves. "We shall make you recite Our revelations, so that you shall forget none of them except as Allah pleases" (87:5). There seems little doubt that from the very beginning of its existence, the *Qur'an* was orally recited (Juynboll 1974). The very word *Qur'an* is said to derive from a root Q-R-', whose basic sense is "proclaim, recite, read aloud" (Graham 2001:30). The emphasis on reciting is also attested to by the fact that there are international *Qur'an* recitation competitions held annually in Egypt, Saudi Arabia, Indonesia, and Malaysia, among other countries. In one held in Cairo in 1994, there were reportedly 187 participants from 102 countries (Chodkiewicz 2001:24). In Kuala Lumpur, forty-five countries have been represented over the years (al Faruqi 1987b:223). The original orality of the *Qur'an* is also signaled by the frequent occurrence of the imperative "Qul!" meaning "Say," which introduces three hundred or so passages (Jones 1994:xxii; Graham 2001:32; for a listing of them, see Kassis 1983:936–43). The written *Qur'an* in that sense is strictly a *textus receptus*, serving as a mnemonic aid intended to facilitate oral performance (cf. Denny 1989; Graham 1987:81–115). As one scholar phrases it, the *Qur'an* "is at once an oral and a written reality" (Nasr 1992:12). Yet despite the widespread consensus that the *Qur'an* was intended from the start to be an oral communication and despite the fact that it continues to be performed orally, it has not really been systematically examined in the light of either oral-formulaic theory (Kellermann 1995:5) or folk narrative theory.

ORAL-FORMULAIC THEORY

It was questions concerning the Homeric epics, the *Iliad* and the *Odyssey*, that provided the initial impetus for oral-formulaic theory. The fundamental issue turned on whether Homer (whoever Homer was) had memorized his epics verbatim, line for line, or whether he had composed them orally on the spot, each time he recited them.

In order to shed light on this matter, Milman Parry (1902–1935) undertook a study of the Serbo-Croatian epic tradition, beginning in 1933 and continuing through the 1930s, accompanied by his then student assistant Albert Lord (1912–1991). Ideally, Parry and Lord would have preferred to have investigated an epic tradition in Greece, the place where Homer presumably lived, but the nearest live epic tradition was available only in the former Yugoslavia. By eliciting and especially re-eliciting the "same" epic from individual epic singers (as well as eliciting the "same" epic from other singers), Parry and Lord discovered that epic singers did not memorize their thousands of lines of narrative exactly word for word. Rather, they composed them anew in each oral performance, relying on a standard repertoire of clichés, commonplaces, stock phrases, or what were termed "formulas." If one imagines an epic as a linear series of boxes or slots, then one can easily picture a talented epic singer filling the slots with appropriate conventional formulas to describe a wedding scene, a bride's beauty, a warrior's armor, and so on. Of course, it was certainly possible for an epic singer, in different recitations, to utilize the identical formula at a given point in the epic, thereby giving the false impression that the epic had indeed been memorized. But the mass of field data accumulated by the Parry-Lord expeditions suggested convincingly that there were, typically, alternative formulas for any particular narrative slot, just one of which was chosen by the raconteur on a given occasion.

In 1949, Albert Lord submitted his doctoral dissertation at Harvard University and it was eventually published in 1960 under the title *The Singer of Tales*. In a way, it was the book that Milman Parry might have written had he not died tragically in 1935. This book is generally regarded as one of the charter statements for oral-formulaic theory.

John Mills Foley in his succinct account (1988) of the prehistory of the oral-formulaic theory notes that there were precursors, precursors acknowledged by Parry himself (Parry 1971:270, n 1). Austrian folklorist Friedrich Krauss (1859–1938), who specialized in the folklore of Yugoslavia, had drawn similar conclusions from his extensive fieldwork carried out with *guslars*. In his 1908 paper, "Vom wunderbaren Guslarengedächtnis," Krauss remarked on the guslar's dependence upon "the fixed formulas from which he neither can nor wishes to vary." Similarly, famed French folklorist Arnold van Gennep (1873–1957) in his 1909 treatise *La Question d'Homère* suggested that "the poems of the guslars consist of a juxtaposition of clichés, relatively few in number and with which it suffices merely to be conversant.... A fine guslar is one who handles these clichés as we play with cards, who orders them differently according to the use he wishes to make of them" (1909:52).

What exactly are these clichés or oral formulas? And how can they be identified? Parry defined the formula as "an expression regularly used, under the same metrical conditions, to express an essential idea" (Parry 1971:13; Lord 1965:30; Foley 1988:24). The most expeditious way of identifying formulas is to note repeated utterances in a given text. An utterance that happens only once could, in theory, be a formula, but without at least a second iteration, such an apparent *hapax legomenon* could not really be definitively labeled a formula. True formulas are, in fact, repeated many, many times, and not just by individual oral poets. Formulas are traditional and are normally employed by all oral poets participating in the performance of a particular genre in a given linguistic or cultural community.

Although the original motivation for the development of oral-formulaic theory may have been to shed light on the composition of the Homeric epics, the theory, once articulated, was applied to many other traditions found in many different time periods and in many different cultures. The basic idea was to see whether or not a particular poem might have originally been orally transmitted before having been committed to written form. Not surprisingly, the notion of "formulaic density as a test of orality" was proposed. If a given poetic work had a sufficient number of formulas, it was argued that this could be regarded as a kind of litmus test for the poem's oral roots (Foley 1988:55). One question, of course, is just how many formulas need to be present in a given work to qualify the work as a product of oral composition. Another theoretical difficulty was the possibility that literate poets might seek to imitate oral style by intentionally inserting actual, or perhaps consciously created, formula-like idioms into their poems (Sowayan 1985:185). In other words, the mere presence of formulas in a text is not necessarily proof positive of oral composition (Wansbrough 1977:48). In any case, opinions varied as to just what the formula density percentage had to be before declaring a particular poem as orally composed. Joseph Duggan, for example, in a 1966 study of thirteen Old French songs, proposed a figure of "20 percent straight formulas" as a minimum threshold figure required to establish orality (Foley 1988:80). Duggan also examined multiple versions of the *Song of Roland* and offered the following conclusion with respect to formula density: "In general, if an Old French narrative poem is less than 20 percent straight repetition, it probably derives from literary, or written, creation. When the formula density exceeds 20 percent, it is strong evidence of oral composition, and the probability rises as the figure increases over 20 percent" (1973:29). Duggan calculated that the *Song of Roland* had a formula density percentage of 35.2, thereby indicating that it was indeed originally an oral poem. While one may well choose to quibble over the apparent arbitrariness of the figure of 20 percent (why not 25 or 30 percent?), the validity of the argument seems sound enough.

The question might be raised as to whether or not oral-formulaic theory can legitimately be applied to Arabic poetry. Linguist Mary Catherine Bateson, daughter of anthropologists Margaret Mead and Gregory Bateson, in her Harvard doctoral dissertation, in which she examined five pre-Islamic Arabic odes, said in unequivocal terms that it could not. After briefly summarizing the Parry-Lord approach, Bateson concluded, "This theory may be rejected for Arabic on the basis of both internal and external evidence" (1970:34). Folklorist Saad Sowayan devotes the last chapter of his important book *Nabati Poetry: The Oral Poetry of Arabia* to the same question of whether or not oral-formulaic theory can legitimately be applied to ancient Arabic poetry (1985:183–208). Although Sowayan acknowledges that verbal formulas "do indeed appear with high frequency in ancient Arabic poetry," he claims that "ancient Arabic poetry is not oral-formulaic" in the sense of the original criteria established by Milman Parry and Albert Lord (1985:206). In contrast, James T. Monroe in his substantial 1972 essay, "Oral Composition in Pre-Islamic Poetry," made a persuasive argument to the contrary. In fact, the oral-formulaic theory seems to have been applied to pre-Islamic Arabic poetry with some success (Zwettler 1976, 1978; Foley 1988:86–88), but to my knowledge it has not hitherto been applied to the *Qur'an*, with the exception of a single essay by Welch (2000) limited just to identifying a very few formulas in what are termed "punishment stories."

With respect to applying oral-formulaic theory to the *Qur'an*, one might legitimately raise the question as to whether or not the theory can be applied to anything other than the epic genre or to poetry. Certainly the theory in *sensu strictu*, at least in terms of its original articulation, referred only to epics, the Homeric and Serbo-Croatian epics in particular. Inasmuch as the *Qur'an* is not an epic and inasmuch as it tends to be regarded as prose rather than poetry—although it could be argued (cf. Gluck 1982) that it does contain poetic features and it is of interest in this context that Muhammad's pagan detractors went so far as to accuse him of being a poet inspired or possessed by a jinn (37:36), as jinn were credited with having the ability to provide supernatural knowledge to prospective poets (Izutsu 1964:169–71; Monroe 1971:36)—one might contend that it would be inappropriate to apply oral-formulaic theory to the *Qur'an*. (Incidentally, the accusation of Muhammad being a soothsayer or a jinn-inspired poet is specifically denied in the *Qur'an* [52:29, 59:42].)

The answer to this would-be objection is that there is no need to limit the oral-formulaic theory to a single genre, namely, the epic, nor need it necessarily be confined solely to poetic discourse. Indeed, the theory has been successfully applied to African American sermons (Rosenberg 1970), among other genres. While the theory would not be applicable to fixed phrase folklore genres such as the proverb or the riddle or to any genre where the wording remains word-for-word identical each time an instance of that genre was employed by an individual, it would be relevant to any genre involving improvisation on the part of a performer. Moreover, I would suggest that oral-formulaic theory could be usefully applied to any genre, oral or, for that matter, even written, in which identifiable formulas are found. Accordingly, one could imagine oral-formulaic studies of such everyday forms as introductions of speakers, graduation addresses, book reviews, obituary notices, personal want ads, and various types of letters, such as letters of condolence and letters of recommendation. With such a broader understanding of oral-formulaic theory, it would not be impossible to apply the theory to the *Qur'an*.

There are several other reasons why oral-formulaic theory as well as other folkloristic theories have not been applied to the *Qur'an*. For one thing, no folklorist wants to be accused of "orientalism." Ever since the publication in 1978 of Edward Said's famous book on the subject in which the accusation was made (and substantiated) that Western scholars tended to force Middle Eastern and Asian cultures into ethnocentric Procrustean Western categories, thereby misinterpreting and misunderstanding those cultures, Western folklorists have been understandably reluctant to consider the *Qur'an* from the perspective of contemporary folkloristic theories (cf. Tibawi 1979; Khalifa 1983; Manzoor 1986, 1987; for representative reasoned critiques of Said's influential book, see Sadik Jalal al-'Azm's "Orientalism and Orientalism in Reverse" [1981], and Bernard Lewis's chapter entitled "The Question of Orientalism" in his book *Islam and the West* [1993:99–118]; for a useful survey of the contributions of five major "orientalists"—I. Goldziher [1850–1921], C. Snouck Hurgronje [1857–1936], C. H. Becker [1876–1933], D. B. Macdonald [1863–1943], and L. Massignon [1883–1962], but not including Theodor Nöldeke [1836–1930]—see Waardenburg 1962).

The rise of orientalism has led to an unfortunate intellectual impasse in the study of the *Qur'an*. Two incompatible worldviews are involved. From the Islamic perspective, Western "orientalist" scholars are unduly obsessed with empirical, objective facts, a bias that leads them to concentrate on various aspects of source criticism, for example, on questions of the historicity of details in the *Qur'an*, or on possible literary borrowings, say, from earlier Jewish or Christian traditions. From the Western "orientalist" perspective, Islamic scholars are so blinded by their faith that they are unable or unwilling to subject the *Qur'an* to any form of so-called "higher criticism," of the sort that has been applied for centuries to Western religious texts such as the Old and New Testaments. Most writings on the *Qur'an* seem to reflect one or the other of these worldviews.

It is certainly not always easy to avoid the charge of indulging in ethnocentric orientalism. For example, to a Westerner, the sound of the *Qur'an* being recited has all the earmarks of a musical performance, not unlike the various forms of cantillation found in Orthodox Jewish religious services, for example. This does not carry any weight with Islamic fundamentalists who adamantly oppose any attempt to use the adjective *musical* in connection with *Qur'an*ic recitation (Farmer 1952:62; Nelson 1985:153, 189; al Faruqi 1987a:14; Bedford 2001; Rasmussen 2001:36). The effort to keep recitation of the *Qur'an* free from any possible influence from secular singing goes back to the early days of Islam (Talbi 1958). One twenty-first-century Western author, in discussing such recitation, chose to use the word *musical* for convenience but acknowledges that if his book were to be translated into Arabic, "the word would have to be edited out" (Cook 2000:84). It is no accident that the few Arab scholars who have dared to call *Qur'an*ic recitation a form of religious music have done so in languages other than Arabic. Yet, even such brave souls readily acknowledge that in the Islamic world, the *Qur'an* is never sung, but rather "recited" or "read aloud" (Touma 1975:87). The cultural logic here is that labeling the *Qur'an*ic recitation "music" would impugn the *Qur'an*'s claim of uniqueness. If the *Qur'an* is truly inimitable, totally unique, and of divine origin, it simply cannot be treated or viewed as comparable to any other object, certainly not a human object. To call its recitation "music" would therefore demean it by classifying it as belonging to a whole range of purely ordinary mundane creations. In 1999 in Lebanon, a singer was ordered to stand trial accused of having sung a blasphemous song. The song was actually a secular one but its text had included a passage from the *Qur'an*. The logic of the charge against the singer was basically this: "It was one thing to quote the *Qur'an*, but to set its words to music—even when they were embedded in a poem—and to accompany them with instruments was 'to go beyond the respect due to God on earth.'" (Bedford 2001:4). One of the rules is that "Instruments are never used as accompaniment for Qur'anic recitation" (al Faruqi 1987a:8) because musical instruments are believed to have been invented by Satan. Another rule is that one may not "recite the *Qur'an* just as he sings a song" because "the *Qur'an* contains God's words and the recitation of the *Qur'an* is an act of worship" (Cetin 1999:118, 120). So it is abundantly clear that "reciting" is not to be confused with "singing," even though the Western ear may be unable to make the distinction and cannot do other than perceive a definite melodic component in *Qur'an*ic recitation. In Indonesia, there does seem to be a slightly more liberal attitude with respect to discussing possible "musical" aspects of *Qur'an* recitation (Rasmussen 2001), but this is definitely not the case in the Arab world. In the latter context, Western scholars find it politically incorrect to consider "this music-which-nobody-calls-music" (Bedford 2001:3). The whole issue turns on a fine line in the spectrum of cultural constructions of perception, a line that, although nearly invisible to the Western eye, is evidently visible, or should we rather say audible, to reciters of the *Qur'an*. A detailed description of a reputed blind reciter in Cairo notes admiringly that he "never crosses the difficult-to-discern line into purely musical expression" (Denny 1980:153).

Another reason for the failure to study the *Qur'an* folkloristically is the special privileged status of that book. So, orientalism considerations aside, the *Qur'an* as a sacred religious charter is simply off limits. So-called "higher criticism" of the kind that has been applied to both the Old and New Testaments is just not deemed acceptable. Arab scholars living in the Arab world run the risk of losing their jobs or worse should they attempt to apply folkloristic methodology to the *Qur'an*, as is suggested by the sad case of Professor Nasr Hamid Abu Zayd cited above—and he was not even a folklorist. Western scholars who are in theory free to study whatever they like tend to value their associations with Arab colleagues and consequently have refrained from examining the *Qur'an* from a folkloristic viewpoint as a matter of respect for their colleagues.

A few scholars have commented on "repeated phrases" in the *Qur'an*. Robson, for example, notes that "Four phrases are most excellent: Glory be to God; Praise be to God; There is no god but God; and God is most great" (1957:43, 46). Robson suggests that such repeated phrases are an echo of the Prophet's method of teaching (47). For that matter, whenever the *Qur'an* is even mentioned, it is usually accompanied by such "exalted appellations" as "The Bounteous, Noble or Honorable," "The Full of Wisdom," "The Glorious," or "The Great or Sublime" (Khalifa 1983:4), all of which could legitimately be considered to be "formulas."

The current project reverses the usual oral-formulaic research effort. Typically, a scholar is seeking to demonstrate the original orality of a text by discerning the presence of "formulas" in the text in question. In other words, the orality of the text is either in doubt or is disputed. In such cases, enumerating the formulas is a methodological technique designed to authenticate the possible or probable oral roots of the text. With the *Qur'an*, we have the opposite situation. It has long been assumed and argued that the *Qur'an* was originally oral. In fact, it is still supposed to be orally performed and transmitted. The initial orality of the *Qur'an* is really not in question, although it has been pointed out that the original oral aspects have tended to be neglected because of the overwhelming domination of the written text (Jones 1996:59). What I hope to show is that this presumed orality is thoroughly attested by the presence of hundreds of formulas contained in the *Qur'an*.

ORAL FORMULAS IN THE *QUR'AN*

Ideally, a true oral-formulaic study of the *Qur'an* should take account of the formulas in Arabic with due attention paid to such poetic features as end or internal rhymes, metrics, assonance, enjambment, and so on (Gluck 1982; for a convincing analysis of a sampling of oral formulas found in pre-Islamic Arabic poems, see Monroe 1972). Lacking the linguistic competence to do so, however, does not necessarily preclude undertaking an oral-formulaic approach. Thanks to the existence of a comprehensive concordance to the *Qur'an* in English, it is possible to identify likely formulas. (The inestimable value of a concordance in facilitating oral-formulaic analysis has long been recognized; see Magoun 1953:459, 461.) In other words, formulas can survive translation from one language to another. Fortunately, Hanna E. Kassis's 1,444-page *A Concordance of the Qur'an*, published in 1983 by the University of California Press, provides an invaluable resource for the identification of probable oral formulas. Although Kassis chose the English rendering of A. J. Arberry in *The Qur'an Interpreted* as the basis for the concordance (rather than other possible translations), this has little or no impact on the search for formulas. Even if a formula is translated differently by different translators, its formulaic status remains easy enough to recognize. So if the sample formulas to be cited in this essay do not correspond exactly in every detail to the wording of the same formulas in particular translations of the *Qur'an*, that would not by any means rule them out as bona fide formulas.

In terms of methodology, the technique for identifying formulas is simply to search for any cliché or phrase that is repeated. Even if such a group of words were repeated only once or twice, that verbal cluster would in theory qualify as a potential formula. For example, in referring to Allah's creation of the heavens, we find two instances of the following phraseology: Allah "created the seven heavens, one above the other" (67:3, 71:15). While it would obviously be a stronger case if there were many more occurrences of this particular collocation of words, the existence of even just two instances points to its formulaic status. It turns out that there are quite a few instances of two iterations of what could be construed as likely authentic formulas. Let us consider the following examples. One is found in the portrayal of someone who rejects idols and believes in Allah as one "who has taken hold of a strong unbreakable handle" (2:256, 31:22) as well as the plea to Allah to "pour out upon us patience" (2:250, 7:126). Allah is also asked to grant his prophets the "tongue of truth" (19:50, 26:84), a felicitous phrase that signifies or guar-

Folklore in the *Qur'an* 25

antees that their words will be held in high repute by future generations. Occurring twice is a stock response to those who make unsubstantiated claims, such as, only Jews and Christians shall enter paradise, or, there are other gods besides Allah: "Produce your proof if what you say is true" (2:111, 27:64, cf. 21:24, 28:75). It should probably be noted that the final conditional segment, "If you speak truly," is a separate and frequently repeated formula in its own right (2:31, 94, 111; 3:168, 183; 6:40, 143; 7:194; 10:38, 48; 11:13, 32; 21:38, 28:49, 29:29, 32:28, 36:48, 44:36, 45:25, 46:4, 56:87, 62:6, 67:25). Upon admission to paradise, the faithful are purged of any residual grudges or hatred: "We shall remove whatever rancor they may have in their hearts" (7:43, 15:47). Among the array of doublets, we note that the important difference between undrinkable salt water and potable water is mentioned in formulaic fashion on two occasions. One of the "two seas" is "sweet and fresh" while the other is "salt and bitter" (25:53, 35:12). Similarly, there are just two illustrations of an idiom (Mir 1989:219) describing the desire of sinners to blow out the flame of Islam: "They would extinguish the light of Allah with their mouths but Allah persists in perfecting His light in spite of the unbelievers" (9:32, 61:8, cf. 66:8). Still another such example is the epithet used to describe the fuel for the fire of Gehenna or hell reserved for unbelievers or sinners. We are told twice that unbelievers should fear the fire "whose fuel is men and stones" (2:24, 66:6). Similarly, we find two or possibly three accounts of the scales of justice on the Day of Judgment: "On that day ... those whose good deeds weigh heavy in the scales shall triumph while those whose deeds are light shall lose their souls" (7:9, 23:103, cf. 101:8). The smallest possible infraction or good deed will be counted "even if it be the weight of [just] one grain of mustard-seed" (21:47, 31:16), this being a formula also found in the New Testament (Matthew 13:31, 17:20, Mark 4:31, Luke 13:19, 17:6). Another hyperbolic formula expressing the ultimate degree of small size also occurs only twice. "Not so much as the weight of an ant on earth or in heaven escapes the notice of Allah" (10:61, 34:3, cf. 4:40, 34:22). Most English translations have "atom" in place of "ant" but the image remains effective with either word. The only variation in the formula itself is that the first instance has "earth and heaven" while the second reverses the order and has "heaven and earth," variation typical of oral tradition (cf. 3:5 and 14:38—according to Kassis 1983:684). Perhaps the most piquant formula expressing the most extreme degree of insignificance involves the thin hairlike membrane of the pit of a date. Speaking of pure believers, the *Qur'an* says, "They shall not be wronged by as much as the husk of a date stone" (4:49, 77; 17:71). The identical formula is also employed to show how little power Allah's rival pagan gods have: "Those you call upon, apart from Him, possess not so much as the husk of a date stone" (35:13).

A formula expressing the smallest possible degree of time describes the time required to wink. The formula, which also is repeated only twice, is "the blinking of an eye," referring to the time required for the coming of the Day of Judgment and to the time required for Allah's commands to be carried out (16:77, 54:50), and the same formula is found in the Bible (1 Corinthians 15:52).

There are likewise only two instances of a description of what will happen to mountains on that same Day of Judgment: "The mountains will be like tufts of carded wool" (70:9, 101:5). Similarly, on that dire occasion, a violent windstorm "swept away men as though they were palm trees pulled out by the roots" (54:20, 69:7). Of course, one could argue that all these instances might be just coincidentally similar, but the fact that there are dozens and dozens of formulas in the *Qur'an*, the vast majority of which are repeated many, many times, would indicate otherwise. For example, the formulaic epithet applied to slaves or captives is typically "what your right hand possesses" (4:3, 24, 25, 36; 16:71, 23:6, 24:31, 33, 58; 30:28, 33:50, 52, 55; 70:30).

There is one caveat, though, with respect to the methodology of locating two or more occurrences of a verbal cluster, and that is the problem of parallel or duplicate passages. The *Qur'an*, like the Bible, is riddled with duplicate passages. Often an entire verse of a particular surah is found nearly verbatim in one or more other surahs (cf. Wansbrough 1977:21–22). Here is an example:

> It is He who has sent forth His Messenger with guidance and the True Faith that He may exalt it above all religions, even though the unbelievers may dislike it. (9:32)
>
> It is He that has sent forth His Messenger with guidance and the True Faith so that he may exalt it above all religions. (48:28)
>
> It is He who has sent forth his Messenger with guidance and the True Faith so that he may exalt it above all religions, even though the unbelievers may dislike it. (61:9)

This is essentially the same passage repeated three times. Therefore one might be tempted to claim that any phrase contained therein would have to count only as a single iteration, at least in terms of hunting for formulas. Incidentally, a modern editor, armed with the "Find" feature on his or her computer, would no doubt have eliminated such duplicate passages as being unnecessarily repetitious. However, since the *Qur'an* is thought to be a sacred text consisting of Allah's own words, it would have been deemed sacrilegious to delete such duplicate passages. This is precisely the logic that prevented the deletion of even longer duplicate passages in the Old and New Testaments (Dundes 1999). Some of the duplicate passages evince slight variation, which is to be expected inasmuch as the *Qur'an* was orally transmitted. For example, as a rebuttal to unbelievers who accused Muhammad of having made up the *Qur'an* himself, we find the following:

> If you doubt what We have revealed to Our servant, produce **one** Surah comparable to it. Call upon your idols to assist you, if what you say be true. (2:23)
>
> If they say: "He invented it himself," say, "Bring me **one** Surah like it. Call on whom you may besides Allah to help you, if what you say be true!" (10:38)

Compare these two passages with one in the very next surah: "If they say: 'He has invented it himself,' say to them: 'Produce **ten** invented Surahs like it. Call on whom you will besides Allah, if what you say be true'" (11:13).

Such variation in number as one versus ten is typical of oral tradition (Dundes 1999:21–37). Another striking example of numerical variation also occurs in consecutive verses:

> Prophet, rouse the faithful to arms. If there are **twenty** steadfast men among you, they shall vanquish **two hundred** and if there are a **hundred**, they shall rout a **thousand** unbelievers. (8:65)
>
> If there are a **hundred** steadfast men among you, they shall vanquish **two hundred**; and if there are a **thousand**, they shall, by God's will, defeat **two thousand**. (8:66)

Here is a partial list of duplicate passages in the *Qur'an*: 2:49, 7:141 and 14:6; 2:60 and 7:160; 2:125 and 22:26; 2:173 and 16:115; 4:43 and 5:6; 6:10, 13:32, and 21:41; 6:17 and 10:107; 6:50 and 11:31; 7:8 and 23:102; 7:24 and 20:123; 7:73 and 11:64; 7:107–124 and 26:32–49; 8:2 and 22:35; 8:13 and 59:4; 9:32 and 61:8; 9:73 and 66:9; 11:37 and 23:27; 11:82 and 15:74; 13:41 and 21:44; 15:19 and 50:7; 15:28–39 and 38:72–83; 15:88 and 20:131; 16:58 and 43:17; 16:66 and 23:21; 17:35 and 26:181–82; 17:48 and 25:9; 17:83 and 41:51; 20:22, 26:33 and 28:32; 20:24 and 79:17; 21:16 and 44:38; 22:62 and 31:30; 26:52 and 44:23; 26:90 and 50:31; 27:80–81 and 30:52–53; 28:60 and 42:36; 29:8 and 46:15; 34:2 and 57:4; 35:40 and 46:4; 38:13 and 50:14; 40:64 and 64:3; 52:40–42, 48 and 68:46–48. (Anyone checking these passages should keep in mind that in different editions/translations of the *Qur'an*, surah line numbers may vary slightly.)

There are many examples of the variations found in apparent duplicate passages. For example, in the allusions to the dramatic episode in which Moses casts down his staff that turns into a serpent, sometimes the formulas are at first glance identical: "And when he saw it slithering like a serpent, he turned and fled, without a backward glance" (27:10, 28:31), but on the other hand, one version has the nobles or leaders of Pharaoh's people warning Pharaoh that Moses is a skillful sorcerer (7:109), while in another version (26:34) it is Pharaoh who makes the identical statement to his nobles or leaders (Elder 1925:258). From the point of view of historicity, presumably either Pharaoh's followers told him or he told his followers. A small point, but precisely what is to be expected when one has several oral traditions recounting the same basic story, as we have previously shown is the case in both the Old and New Testaments (Dundes 1999).

Sometimes it is somewhat difficult to distinguish between duplicate passages, such as the retellings of the stories of Noah or Moses, and repeated formulaic segments. For example, consider the following verse: "Who is more wicked than he who invents a lie against Allah or denies His revelations?" (6:21). This "formula" occurs at least ten more times in the *Qur'an,* including thrice more in the sixth surah (6:93, 6:144, 6:157), plus once in the seventh (7:37), once in the tenth (10:17), once in the eleventh (11:18), once in the eighteenth (18:15), once in the twenty-ninth (29:68), once in the thirty-ninth (39:32), and finally once in the sixty-first (61:7). In two of the ten instances, the formula is followed by yet another formula: "Is there not a home in Gehenna [Hell] for the unbelievers?" (29:68, 39:32).

Similarly, as noted above, we have "It is He who has sent forth His Messenger with guidance and the True Faith so that he may exalt it above all religions" repeated three times and in two of the instances, this formula is followed by "though the idolaters abhor it" (9:33, 61:9), a formula that also appears in an immediately preceding verse (9:32, 61:8).

One could perhaps justifiably argue that duplicate texts should **not** be counted as single iterations of a given formula. On the contrary, the fact that whenever a given narrative element appears, it always utilizes the same formula could be construed as a positive indication that oral-formulaic technique is involved. For example, there are numerous allusions to the story of Moses and in almost all of them, there is a formula in which the Pharaoh threatens Moses and the Israelites by saying that he will "cut off their hands and feet on alternate sides" (5:33, 7:124, 20:71, 26:49). Similarly, there is a repeated reference to Allah's assisting the Israelites in their escape from Pharaoh: "We (He) delivered you from Pharaoh's people who had oppressed you cruelly, slaughtering your sons and sparing only your daughters" (2:49, 7:127, 141; 14:6, 28:4). There are numerous occurrences of the formula that "We gave to Moses the Book," presumably referring to the Torah (2:53, 87; 6:154, 11:110, 17:2, 23:49, 25:35, 28:43, 32:23, 41:45).

The way oral formulas work is that whenever a particular situation arises in a narrative, there is a set of formulas that can be utilized in that situation. For example, if a sword is being described, no matter who the wielder of the sword might be, the same formula emphasizing the sharpness of the blade might be appropriately employed. A good example of this sort of generic formula in the *Qur'an* may be seen in the stock phrase occurring in connection with different figures in the Old Testament, namely, Joseph, Lot, David and Solomon, and Moses. Allah bestowed on all of these prophets "wisdom and knowledge" (12:22, 21:74, 21:79, 28:14). In the cases of Joseph and Moses, the formulaic description includes the further detail that these qualities were given when each "had attained his maturity" (12:22, 28:14). There can be no doubt that "wisdom and knowledge" qualifies as a genuine formula.

Sometimes formulas, in contrast, are associated with just one individual and are not so easily transferable. In Homer's epics, we had "ox-eyed Hera," "cloud-gathering Zeus," "fleet-footed Achilles," "wily Odysseus," "rosy-fingered Eos [dawn]," and the "wine-dark sea," among many other particularistic formulas. Odysseus is never "fleet-footed" and Achilles is never "wily." The important distinction between distinctive or "particularistic" epithets used in connection with one specific individual as opposed to so-called generic epithets that could be employed with a variety of characters was made early on by Milman Parry in his 1928 dissertation, "The Traditional Epithet in Homer" (Parry 1971:145).

An illustration of a particularistic formula in the *Qur'an* is afforded by a description of Abraham. The *Qur'an* insists that "Abraham was neither Jew nor Christian, but rather a Muslim" (3:67), and it is clear that he was very much admired for his adherence to monotheism and his refusal to indulge in polytheism. The formula in question is: "Abraham the upright. He was no idolater" (2:135, 3:67, 95; 6:161, 16:120, 123; cf. 4:125, 6:79). It does not appear to be associated with any other specific personage mentioned in the *Qur'an* but is thought, rather, to be an ideal to be emulated (10:105).

By far the greatest number of formulas consist of attributes, often as doublets, ascribed to the Supreme Being. Allah is all-mighty and all-wise; Allah is all-knowing, all-wise; Allah is the all-high, the all-great; Allah is all-sufficient, all-laudable; Allah is all-forgiving, all-compassionate; Allah is all-hearing, all-seeing; Allah is all-embracing, all-knowing; Allah is all-knowing, all-powerful. Allah is the One, the Omnipotent. Such formulas, far too numerous to count, permeate the *Qur'an* throughout. One estimate is that there are ninety-nine such "beautiful names" describing Allah, further noting that "A common feature of *Qur'an*ic style is to have a verse ending with two names of God" (Watt 1970:152). Welch claims that the phrase "Allah is all-forgiving, all-compassionate" occurs more than fifty times as a rhyme formula (2000:78). Allah is described repeatedly as "Lord of the Universe (or of the Worlds or of all Being)" (1:2, 2:131, 5:28, 6:45, 71, 162; 7:54, 67, 104; 10:10, 37; 26:23, 47, 77, 98, 109, 127, 145, 164, 180, 192; 27:8, 27:44, 37:87, 182; 39:75, 40:64, 65, 66; 41:9, 43:46, 45:36, 56:80, 59:16, 69:43, 81:29, and 83:6). Some formulas occur much less frequently: "Allah is gracious and aware" (22:63, 31:16, 33:34). The crucial point is that it matters not whether a formula is repeated thrice or fifty times. What is important to keep in mind in the present context is that an identified formula is a formula, regardless of its frequency of occurrence.

There is a well-known anecdote, perhaps apocryphal (Zakaria 1991:67), that suggests that some of these formulaic attributes of Allah might be interchangeable. As the story goes, one of the official amanuenses, named Abdollah b. Sa'd b. Abi Sarh, charged with recording Muhammad's recitation of the divine revelation, had the habit of changing the closing words of verses, albeit with the Prophet's consent. In one instance, for example, when Muhammad said "And Allah is mighty and wise," the scribe suggested substituting "knowing and wise" instead (Dashti 1985:98). Supposedly Muhammad readily accepted the emendation, claiming that "So it has been revealed" (al Imam 1998:60). Abdollah eventually renounced Islam because he felt that if the revelations were truly from Allah, they should not be able to be altered by the editorial interference of a mere scribe. From the perspective of oral-formulaic theory, what is significant in this anecdote is Muhammad's apparent judgment that one formula may justifiably be substituted for another.

Allah's various powers are also articulated in formulaic fashion. Allah created the heavens and the earth (6:14, 79; 7:54, 10:3, 12:101, 14:10, 19, 32; 17:99, 29:44, 61; 30:8, 31:25, 32:4, 35:1, 39:38, 46; 42:11, 45:22, 46:33, cf. 2:117, 6:101); to Allah belongs the kingdom of the heavens and the earth (2:107, 3:189, 5:17, 18, 40, 120; 7:158, 9:116, 24:42, 25:2, 39:44, 42:49, 43:85, 45:27, 48:14, 57:2, 5; 85:9); "Unto Him belong the keys of the heavens and the earth" (39:63, 42:12); Allah is "Lord of the East and the West" (26:28, 70:40, 73:9); Allah creates what He will (3:47, 24:45, 28:68, 30:54, 42:49); Allah has knowledge of all your actions (3:121, 156; 4:108, 8:47, 11:92, 24:28, 30, 41; 27:88, 42:25, 47:30, 63:11, 64:8); Allah is aware of what you do (2:234, 271; 3:153, 180; 4:94, 128, 135; 5:8, 9:16, 11:111, 24:53, 31:29, 33:2, 48:11, 57:10, 58:3, 11, 13; 59:18, 63:11, 64:8); Allah sees the things you do (2:96, 110, 233, 237, 265; 3:156, 163; 5:71, 8:39, 72; 33:9, 41:40, 48:24, 49:18, 57:4, 60:3, 64:2); Allah hears all and knows all (2:137, 181; 8:42, 53, 61; 29:60, 40:20); Allah has knowledge of everything (2:29, 231, 282; 4:176, 5:97, 6:101, 8:75, 24:35, 29:62, 33:40, 54; 42:12, 48:26, 49:16, 57:3, 58:7, 64:11); Allah has power over all things (2:20, 106, 109, 148, 259, 284; 3:29, 165, 189; 4:85, 133; 5:17, 19, 40; 8:41, 9:39, 11:4, 16:77, 24:45, 29:20, 33:27, 35:1, 41:39, 48:21, 59:6, 64:1, 65:12, 66:8, 67:1); Allah has knowledge of your innermost thoughts (3:119, 154; 5:7, 8:43, 11:5, 31:23, 35:38, 39:7, 42:24, 57:6, 64:4, 67:13); Allah makes clear His revelations to mankind (2:187, 221, 242, 266; 3:103, 118; 5:89, 24:18, 58, 59, 61); Allah loves not the arrogant and boastful (4:36, 31:18, 57:23); Allah loves not the evil-doers (3:57, 140; 5:64, 28:77, 42:40); Allah loves the good-doers (2:195, 3:134, 148; 5:13, 93); Allah is the protector of the believers (2:257, 3:68, 47:11); Allah loves those who are just (5:42, 49:9, 60:8); Allah is never unjust to His servants (3:182, 8:51, 22:10, 41:46, 50:29); Allah's grace is infinite (2:105, 3:74, 174; 8:29, 57:21, 29; 62:4); Allah does not guide the evil-doers (5:51, 67, 108; 6:144, 9:19, 24, 37, 80, 109; 16:107, 39:3, 40:28, 46:10, 61:5, 7; 62:5, 63:6); Allah is swift at reckoning (2:202, 3:19, 199; 5:4,

13:41, 14:51, 24:39, 40:17); Allah is severe in retribution (2:196, 211; 3:11, 5:2, 98; 8:13, 25, 48, 52; 13:6, 40:22, 59:4, 7); Allah, if he pleases, can remove you and replace you with others in your stead (4:133, 5:54, 6:133, 14:19, 35:16). This latter formula is reminiscent of Allah's power of abrogation whereby He is able to negate one statement in the *Qur'an* and replace it with a better one. It is also echoed in a domestic incident in the life of Muhammad, when two of his wives were warned not to conspire against him: "If you conspire against him, know that Allah is his protector. . . . It may well be that if he divorces you, Allah will give him in your place better wives than yourselves" (66:5).

The idiom "All that is in the heavens and the earth gives glory to Allah" functions as an opening formula for several surahs (57:1, 59:1, 61:1, 62:1, 64:1) as noted by Welch (2000:77), but it also appears near the end of the fifty-ninth surah (59:24). "Praise be to Allah" (1:2, 6:1, 18:1, 34:1, 35:1) also serves as an opening formula but it too occurs elsewhere (6:45, 7:43, 10:10, 14:39, 16:75, 17:111, 23:28, 27:15, 59, 93; 29:63, 31:25, 35:34, 37:182, 39:29, 74, 75; 40:65, 45:36). Most formulas are by no means limited to the initial position in a surah and can in fact be found anywhere in a given surah. We can see this in remarking that all actions are carried out "by the leave of Allah" (2:97, 102, 249, 251; 3:49, 145, 166; 4:64, 8:66, 10:100, 13:38, 14:11, 35:32, 40:78, 58:10, 59:5, 64:11). This demonstrates the extraordinary flexibility of formulas with respect to where they may appear in a given surah.

Some of the powers of Allah are described in quite eloquent fashion: "Allah makes the night enter into the day and makes the day enter into the night" (3:27, 22:61, 31:29, 35:13, 57:6) is a more poetic image than simply being credited for "the alternation of night and day" (2:164, 3:190, 10:6, 23:80, 45:5). Another lyrical formula of the same ilk is "Allah made the night for you to rest therein and the day to give you light so that you could see" (10:67, 27:86, 28:73, 40:61, cf. 6:96). "Allah pressed the sun and the moon into His service, compelling them to run in their predetermined orbits" (13:2, 14:33, 29:61, 31:29, 35:13, 39:5). The sun and moon are further described as "each swimming in a sky" (21:33, 36:40). The reference to the sun and moon is consistent with the positive value of light as opposed to shadow or darkness. "Allah leads them [believers] out of darkness into light" (2:257, 5:16, 14:1, 5; 33:43, 57:9).

One might think that "night and day" and "sun and moon" are virtually natural formulaic pairs, but it may be worth remarking that the combination of these two pairs, especially if they are in the same sequence, could be construed as constituting a formula. Consider the following three passages: "He has made subject to you the night and the day, and the sun and the moon" (16:12, cf. 14:33), "It is He who created the night and the day, the sun and the moon" (21:33), and "Among His signs are the night and the day, the sun and the moon" (41:37).

Weather also falls under Allah's domain. He is acknowledged as the one who dispatches the winds presaging the arrival of blessed rain. "It is He who sends forth the winds as harbingers of His mercy" (7:57, 25:48, 27:63). "It is Allah who sends forth the winds that stir up the clouds" (30:48, 35:9) and then gathers up the clouds, piling them up, or breaking them up so that one "can see rain(drops) issuing from the midst of them" (24:43, 30:48). Speaking of mercy, it is said of Allah, "Of all those who show mercy, You are the most merciful" (7:151, 12:64, 92; 21:83, 23:109, 118). Allah's control of heavenly phenomena is paralleled by his domination over the movements of earthly objects. For example, "Ships run upon the sea at His command" (2:164, 14:32, 30:46, 45:12).

Other characteristic powers of Allah are stated in more general, matter-of-fact terms: "That is easy enough for Allah" (4:30, 169; 22:70, 29:19, 33:19, 30; 35:11, 57:22, 64:7, cf. 19:9, 21; 30:27). "Allah is the best of providers" (5:114, 22:58, 23:72, 34:39, 62:11, cf. 5:114). "Allah gives abundantly to whom He will and sparingly to whom He pleases" (13:26, 17:30, 28:82, 29:62, 30:37, 34:36, 39; 39:52, 42:12). "Allah does not fail to reward the righteous" (3:171, 7:170, 9:120, 11:115, 12:56, 90; 18:30). "My reward comes only from Allah" (4:100, 10:72, 11:29, 34:47, 42:40). However, most of Allah's attributes tend to be succinct, terse formulas: "Knower of the hidden and the visible" (6:73, 13:9, 23:92, 32:6, 39:46, 59:22, 64:18). A similar formula attests to Allah's ability to know both what unbelievers keep secret and what they say publicly: "Allah has knowledge of what they conceal and what they reveal" (2:33, 77;

3:29, 5:99, 11:5, 14:38, 16:19, 23; 24:29, 27:25, 74; 28:69, 33:54, 36:76, 64:4). Allah's omniscience encompasses both the past and the future. "He knows what has been before them and what shall be after them" (2:255, 20:110, 21:28, 22:76).

Allah's integrity is affirmed by the claim that "Allah suffices as a witness between me and you" (6:19, 10:29, 13:43, 17:96, 29:52, 46:8), this latter formula being analogous to the one in English, "As God is my witness." Nothing escapes Allah's notice. "Allah is witness of all things" (22:17, 58:6, 85:9). Allah also serves as witness in the classic proclamation of faith: "Allah bears witness that there is no god except Him" (3:18, 37:35, 47:19). Allah's power is verbal insofar as he can create by fiat: "When He decrees a thing, He need only say 'Be' and it is" (2:117, 3:47, 59; 6:73, 16:40, 19:35, 36:82, 40:68). Allah's omnipotence makes Him immune from human attack. Even if some of the faithful should backslide, "they cannot harm Allah in the least" (3:176, 11:57, 47:32). Backsliding, actually, is something that does anger Allah and He refuses to forgive "those who disbelieve after they have believed" (3:90, 4:137, 16:106, 63:3).

Satan, in contrast, has many fewer formulaic attributes. "Satan made their foul deeds seem fair to them" (6:43, 8:48, 16:63, 27:24, 29:38, 35:8, 47:14, cf. 3:14, 9:37, 40:37). And Satan is labeled an "acknowledged enemy (foe)" (2:168, 208; 6:142, 7:22, 12:5, 17:53, 35:6, 36:60, 43:62). When Allah ordered all the angels to prostrate themselves before Adam, "they all prostrated themselves except Iblis" (2:34, 7:11, 15:31, 17:61, 18:50, 20:116). (Iblis is the name often used in the *Qur'an* for Satan, clearly derived from "diabolos," in the same way that Issa derives from "Jesus.") Sometimes the same formula can be used with both Satan and Allah. So Satan "enjoins lewdness" (2:268, cf. 24:21), while Allah "forbids lewdness" (16:90), and similarly Satan "enjoins lewdness and bids you assert about Allah what you know not" (2:169), while Allah "does **not** enjoin lewdness. Would you tell of Allah what you know not?" (7:28, cf. 10:68). Incidentally, the formula "but most men know not" is a frequently appearing indictment of man's ignorance of Allah's holy word (7:187, 8:34, 12:21, 40, 68; 16:38, 75;

28:13, 57; 30:6, 30; 34:28, 36; 39:49, 44:39, 45:26). Allah definitely aimed His message at what he considered "men of understanding" (2:179, 197, 269; 3:7, 190; 5:100, 12:111, 13:19, 14:52, 38:29, 43; 39:9, 18, 21; 40:54, 65:10). Such "men of understanding" would presumably know what to do in the event of an effort by Satan to lead them astray. "If Satan tries to tempt you, seek refuge in Allah" (7:200, 41:36).

The formulaic phrase often used to refer to both Jews and Christians is "People of the Book" (3:64, 65, 69, 70, 71, 72, 75, 98, 99, 110, 113, 199; 4:153, 159, 171; 5:15, 19, 59, 65, 68, 77; 29:46, 33:26, 57:29, 59:2, 11; 98:1, 6). Jews are frequently addressed or designated as "Children of Israel" (2:40, 47, 83, 122, 211, 246; 3:49, 93; 5:12, 32, 70, 72, 78, 110; 7:105, 134, 137, 138; 10:90, 93; 17:2, 4, 101, 104; 20:47, 80, 94; 26:17, 22, 59, 197; 27:76, 32:23, 40:53, 43:59, 44:30, 45:16, 46:10, 61:6, 14), a formula also found repeatedly in the Old Testament.

Muhammad's most common epithet is as "Messenger of Allah" (33:40, 48:29) and accordingly we find one of the related formulas to be, "It is the duty of the Prophet to deliver the Message" (5:92, 99; 16:35, 24:54, 29:18, 42:48, 64:12). Muhammad insisted, "I am only a mortal like you" (18:110, 41:6), and that Allah had sent messengers prior to him: "We sent messengers before you" (3:183, 13:38, 17:77, 30:47, 40:78, 43:45). Noah was one such messenger: "We sent Noah to his people" (7:59, 11:25, 23:23, 29:14, 71:1).

Muhammad is instructed more than once by Allah to "give good tidings to believers" (2:25, 223; 9:112, 10:2, 87; 33:47, 61:13). He also represents himself as "no more than a warner" (7:188, 27:92, 34:46, 35:23, 38:65, 46:9, 67:26), bearing clear warnings from Allah. The faithful are supposed to "believe in Allah and His Messenger" (4:136, 152, 171; 7:158, 9:86, 24:47, 62; 48:9, 13; 49:15, 57:19, 21; 58:4, 61:11, 64:8), and the veracity of His message is not to be questioned: "The truth is from your Lord, so be not of those who doubt" (2:147, 3:60, 6:114, 10:94).

Unbelievers are described in many different ways. They badly underestimate Allah. "They measure not Allah according to His true measure" (6:91, 22:74, 39:67). Moreover, they are depicted as unwisely "seeking the chance worldly goods of this life" (4:94, 7:169, 8:67, 24:33). As a result, "Their works have come to mean nothing in this world as well as in the world to come" (2:217, 3:22, 9:69). They are also characterized as fickle, turning to Allah only in times of crisis, but then forgetting Him once the crisis is past: "When man is afflicted with adversity, he turns to Allah and calls upon Him" (10:12, 16:53, 30:33, 39:8, 49; cf. 41:51). They are described as frequently swearing that if such and such occurred, they would become believers: "And they swear by Allah the most solemn oaths" (5:53, 6:109, 16:38, 24:53, 35:42), but they are insincere. They use these oaths simply to mask their faithlessness. "They made their oaths to serve as a cover" (58:16, 63:2).

Unbelievers are invariably contrasted with believers who "enjoin good and forbid evil" (3:104, 110, 114; 7:157, 9:71, 112; 22:41, 31:17). The flexibility of this formula permits portraying unbelievers as those who "enjoin evil and forbid good" (9:67). Unbelievers are also chastised for keeping "believers from the path of Allah and seeking to make it crooked" (3:99, 7:45, 86, 11:19, 14:3), as well as "selling Allah's revelations for a paltry price" (2:174, 3:77, 187, 199; 9:9, cf. 2:41, 79; 5:44, 106; 16:95). With respect to the path of Allah, believers were supposed to "Follow the straight path" (10:89, 11:112, 41:30, 42:15, 46:13). Indeed, one of the reasons for Allah's revelations or signs is so "ye may be guided aright" (2:53, 150; 3:103, 7:158, 21:31, 23:49, 32:3, 43:10). The signs are therefore primarily directed to "every steadfast, appreciative person" (14:5, 31:31, 34:19, 42:33). A rhetorical question asks whether those who plan evil deeds can be certain "that Allah will not cause the earth to swallow them" (16:45, 17:68, 34:9, 67:16, cf. 28:81, 29:40) or unleash "a whirlwind shower of stones" (17:68, 29:40, 54:34, 67:17). One possible illustration of Allah's control over nature might be when an earthquake struck a group of sinners so that "in the morning they were found dead, face down, in their homes" (7:78, 91; 11:67, 94; 29:37).

One reason why Allah is not well disposed toward unbelievers is that they consistently ignore the messages He sends them. When "Their Messengers come to them with clear signs [of Allah's power]" (7:101, 14:9, 30:9, 35:25, 40:83), they stubbornly choose to persist in their disbelief. Allah therefore has little sympathy for unbelievers, preferring to "leave them in their rebelliousness wandering blindly" (2:15, 6:110, 7:186, 10:11, 23:75).

Unbelievers were not just blind, they were described as being "deaf, dumb, and blind" (2:18, 171; 17:97, cf. 6:39, 8:22). There is another striking tripartite formula involving disability: "There is no blame for the blind, no blame for the lame, and no blame for the sick" (24:61, 48:17), such tripartition being a standard formulaic feature as in Allah's creating mankind with "ears, eyes, and hearts" (16:78, 23:78, 32:9, 67:23, cf. 46:26). Several instances of this last formula are followed by one complaining that unbelievers are not properly grateful for having received these critical body parts: "Little thanks you give" (23:78, 32:9, 67:23), although it does occur elsewhere (7:10).

Unbelievers were doomed and were beyond redemption. "Humiliating punishment awaits the unbelievers" (2:90, 3:178, 4:14, 37, 102, 151; 22:57, 31:6, 33:57, 45:9, 58:5, 16), "Neither their wealth nor their children will help them in the least against Allah. They shall be fuel for the fire" (3:10, 116; 34:37, 58:17; cf. 26:88, 71:21).

The utter hopelessness of the fate of the unbelievers is succinctly summarized in a pithy formula, perhaps one of the most familiar of all those found in the *Qur'an*: "Nor will they enter Paradise until the camel passes through the eye of the needle" (7:39). This, of course, means "never" (Mir 1989:369). Not only is this formula cognate with one uttered earlier by Jesus, referring to the unlikelihood of a rich person entering heaven: "It is easier for a camel to go through the eye of a needle, than for rich man to enter into the kingdom of God" (Matthew 19:24, Mark 10:25, Luke 18:25), but it is an example of a standard proverbial genre consisting of "locutions for never" (Taylor 1949). (For a sample of the considerable scholarship on this particular expression, see Aicher 1908; Minear 1942; Tritton 1971; Watt 1972; Oberhuber 1985; Asmussen 1986.) One etymological theory argues that the Greek words *kamelos* (camel) and *kamilos* (anchor rope) were confused or mistranslated, suggesting that the "original" expression involved putting a rope, not a camel, through the eye of a needle. An analogous discussion involves the Arabic words *jamal* (camel) and *jummal* (ship's rope) (Watt 1972:156), but either way, it is surely an apt metaphorical articulation of the slim chances of any unbeliever gaining access to heaven.

Some of the other more sentential formulas have the air of aphorisms. "No soul shall bear another's burden" (6:164, 17:15, 35:18, 39:7, 53:38). "On no soul does Allah place a burden greater than it can bear" (2:286, 6:152, 7:42, 23:62, cf. 2:233, 65:7). "The life of this world is but a sport and a diversion" (6:32, 70; 7:51, 29:64, 47:36, 57:20). "Are a blind man and a seeing man equal?" (6:50, 13:16, 35:19, 40:58). "Is darkness equal to light?" (13:16, 35:20). (These last two formulas appear to be related to a standard folkloristic genre known as either a "pointed rhetorical question" [Dundes 1967:29] or a "sarcastic interrogative affirmative" or "negative" [Doyle 1977]. The genre is an ancient one going back to Sumerian times—examples include "Can one conceive without intercourse?" and "Can one get fat without eating?" [Kramer 1959:121]. A modern affirmative would be "Is the Pope Catholic?" while a negative would be "Does a chicken have lips?") "Counter evil with good" (23:96, 41:34, cf. 11:116). "Truth has come and Falsehood has departed" (17:81, 34:49). "O my people, you act to the best of your ability; I will act to the best of mine" (6:135, 11:93, 121; 39:39). In another expression of reciprocity, "Allah is well pleased with them, and they are well-pleased with Him" (5:119, 9:100, 58:22, 98:8).

Occasionally, there are basic principles of Islam that are expressed as an aphoristic formula: "Celebrate the praise of thy Lord before sunrise and before sunset" (20:130, 50:39) or "Perform the prayer and pay the alms" (2:3, 43, 83, 110, 177, 277; 4:77, 162; 5:12, 55; 8:3, 9:5, 11, 18, 71; 13:22, 14:31, 21:73, 22:35, 78; 24:37, 56; 27:3, 31:4, 33:33, 42:38, 58:13, 73:20, 98:5). Believers were expected to give a portion of what Allah furnished them as alms. "Expend of that which We have provided them" (2:3, 254; 4:39, 22:35, 28:54, 32:16, 36:47, 42:38, 63:10, 65:7). There are additional formulas associated with the giving of alms. One is urged to do so both "in secret and in public" (2:274, 13:22, 14:31, 16:75, 35:29). One should also "give to kinsmen what is due them and give to the needy and to wayfarers" (2:177, 215; 4:36,

8:41, 17:26, 30:38, cf. 59:7). Another formula having to do with alms insists that a portion of one's wealth "should be shared with the beggar and the outcast" (51:19, 70:24–25). Believers were cautioned not to hoard their riches (as they would become the heavy fetters that would weigh them down on Judgment Day) or to stint in any way in giving charity to Allah because ultimately everything in existence is the property of Allah. "To Allah belongs the heritage of the heavens and the earth" (3:180, 57:10).

There are other Islamic principles expressed in formulaic fashion. One might mention a divine dictum, such as "Obey Allah, and the Messenger" (3:32, 132; 4:59, 5:92, 8:1, 20, 46; 24:54, 33:33, 47:33, 58:13, 64:12), a request that was often acknowledged: "We hear, and obey" (2:285, 4:46, 5:7, 24:51), a formula that is parodied (Mir 1989:174) by unbelievers, "We hear but disobey" (2:93, 4:46).

Disobedience could result in dire consequences: "I fear, if I disobey my Lord, the punishment of a dreadful day" (6:15, 10:15, 39:13). There are plenty of warnings: "I fear for you the punishment of a dreadful day" (7:59, 11:26, 84; 26:135, 46:21). A number of other formulas refer to that same dreadful day, Judgment Day, such as "the Trumpet shall be blown" (6:73, 18:99, 20:102, 23:101, 27:87, 36:51, 39:68, 50:20, 69:13, 74:8, 78:18). Another is "upon the day when the hour is come" (30:12, 14, 55, 40:46, 45:27) plus one that affirms its inevitability: "the hour is coming, no doubt of it" (22:7, 40:59, 43:61, 45:32, cf. 18:21, 42:18). Nations and individuals had predestined term limits and when the final moment came, they "shall not delay it for an hour, nor shall they go ahead of time" (7:34, 10:49, 16:61, 34:30, cf. 15:5, 23:43).

The faithful were expected to "believe in Allah and the Last Day" (2:8, 62, 126, 177, 228, 232, 264; 3:114, 4:38, 59, 162; 5:69, 9:18, 19, 29, 44, 99; 24:2, 65:2, cf. 33:21, 60:6). When that day comes, "unto Him you shall all be gathered" (2:203, 3:158, 5:96, 6:38, 72; 8:24, 23:79, 58:9, 67:24). On the Last Day, differences between groups, Jews and Christians, believers and unbelievers, will be judged by Allah. "Allah shall judge between them on the Day of Resurrection" (2:113, 4:141, 10:93, 16:124, 22:17, 69; 32:25, 45:17). Unbelievers could ignore the coming of the Last Day at their peril. "Let them [unbelievers] play and chatter away until they face the day that they are threatened with" (43:83, 70:42, cf. 6:91). "That punishment at which they scoffed shall engulf them" (6:10, 11:8, 16:34, 21:41, 39:48, 40:83, 45:33, 46:26). "Are they waiting for the Hour to come to them suddenly when they least expect it?" (12:107, 43:66, 47:18, cf. 6:31, 22:55, 26:202, 29:53, 39:55). On that fateful day, "Every soul shall be paid back for what it did. None shall be wronged" (2:281, 3:25, 161; 11:111, 14:51, 16:111, 39:70, 40:17, 45:22, 46:19). Still, the faithful have no real reason to fear, according to a rhetorical question: "Shall any be destroyed other than the evil-doers?" (6:47, 46:35). But they must be patient with respect to participating in the event wherein the evil-doers receive their punishment and they receive their just reward. Muhammad himself must do the same: "Wait then, We are waiting with you" (6:158, 7:71, 10:20, 102; 11:122).

Even food taboos are articulated in formulaic fashion: "He has forbidden you carrion, blood, and the flesh of swine; also any flesh that is consecrated to gods other than Allah" (2:173, 5:3, 6:145, 16:115), some of which echoes passages in Leviticus (3:17, 11:7–8, 32). If, however, anyone is forced by necessity, for example, the threat of starvation, to eat any of these substances, so long as he doesn't actually crave them or doesn't willfully intend to disobey the taboo, he is deemed not guilty of any sin by a forgiving Allah: "Whoso is constrained, not desiring nor transgressing, no sin shall be upon him" (2:173, 6:145, 16:115). The prohibition against eating certain substances is opposed to the formulaic exhortation to "eat of the lawful and good things that Allah has provided for you" (2:168, 5:88, 7:32, 16:114, cf. 7:160, 20:81).

The faithful were told "not to corrupt the land with evil" (2:60, 7:74, 85; 11:85, 26:183, 29:36). There was definite pressure to respect the awesome power of Allah: "O believers. Fear Allah" (2:278, 5:35, 8:29, 9:119, 33:70, 57:28, 59:18). A repeated question asks: "Will you not fear Allah?" (7:65, 10:31, 23:23, 32, 87; 26:106, 124, 142, 161, 177; 37:124). Believers were asked to "serve none but Allah" (2:83, 3:64, 11:2, 26; 17:23, 41:14, 46:21) and abide by his laws; "These are the limits set by Allah" (2:187, 229; 4:13, 58:4, 65:1). At the same time, believers were urged to be grateful for Allah's beneficence. They were often given the reminder: "Remember the favor Allah has bestowed upon you" (2:231, 3:103, 5:7, 20; 14:6, 33:9, 35:3), and they were expected to "seek His bounty and give thanks" (16:14, 30:46, 45:12). Allah's aid is infinite and indispensable: "If you try to count Allah's favors, you will not be able to number them" (14:34, 16:18) and "You have none besides Allah to protect or help you" (2:107, 120; 9:116, 29:22, 33:17, 42:31).

There is also an underlying governing rule: "In Allah let believers put their trust" (3:122, 160; 5:11, 9:51, 14:11, 58:10, 64:13). In a variant, "In Allah, let all the trusting put their trust" (12:67, 14:12, 39:38). And that is why true believers repeatedly hear the formula: "Put thy trust in Allah" (3:159, 4:81, 5:23, 8:61, 10:84, 11:123, 27:79, 33:3, 48). On several occasions, this latter formula is immediately followed by "Allah suffices as a guardian" (4:81, 33:3, 48), although this formula also is found elsewhere (4:132, 171; 17:65). One reason to trust Allah is that "Allah's promise is true" (4:122, 10:55, 18:98, 28:13, 30:60, 31:33, 35:5, 40:55, 77; 45:32, 46:17). This is in marked contrast to Satan. "Satan makes them promises only to deceive them" (4:120, 17:64). The *Qur'an* tries to warn believers about Satan's ability to delude and dissemble. "Let not the Arch-Deceiver deceive you about Allah" (31:33, 35:5, cf. 57:14). Believers are exhorted not to follow the devil's path. "Do not walk in the footsteps of Satan" (2:168, 208; 6:142, 24:21), and when they do walk, they should do so humbly: "Walk not on the earth exultantly" (17:37, 31:18).

Another Islamic principle expressed in formulaic fashion is the idea that sinners are accountable for their own sins. "Whosoever goes astray, it is only to his own loss" (10:108, 17:15, 39:41). "Whoever does evil, it is to his own loss" (41:46, 45:15). "Every soul is hostage of its own deeds" (52:21, 74:38). There is a formula that very well encapsulates the sinners' self-incrimination. The sins or evil deeds they commit in life are somehow sent on ahead to Allah prior to Judgment Day and this is accomplished by the sinners' own hands. So it is on the basis of "what their own hands have sent on ahead" (2:95, 3:182, 4:62, 8:51, 18:57, 22:10, 28:47, 30:36, 42:48, 62:7, 78:40, cf. 42:30) that the final judgment is rendered. This idea of the sinners' responsibility for their own plight is also expressed as "Allah did not wrong them, they wronged themselves" (3:117, 9:70, 10:44, 11:101, 16:33, 118; 29:40, 30:9, 43:76). On the other hand, there is some indication that Allah does bear some responsibility for the acts of sinners: "Allah leads astray whomsoever He will" (6:39, 13:27, 14:4, 35:8, 74:31). (Incidentally, the phase *whom(soever) He will* is definitely a formula, just as *had Allah willed* is [Kassis 1983:1154–58].) Allah discusses His stratagem for those who have rejected His revelations: "We will lead them step by step to ruin by means of which they know not and though I give them respite, My scheme will prove effective" (7:182–83, 68:44–45). Once having gone astray, sinners have little chance for success. "Whomsoever Allah leads astray, he shall have no guide" (13:33, 39:23, 36; 40:33). "Surely the wrongdoers shall never prosper" (6:21, 135; 10:17, 12:23, 28:37, cf. 23:117, 28:82), this in contrast to believers: "They are the prosperers" (2:5, 3:104, 7:8, 157; 9:88, 23:102, 24:51, 28:67, 30:38, 31:5, 58:22, 59:9, 64:16). Believers can expect "forgiveness and a generous provision" (8:4, 74; 22:50, 24:26, 34:4, cf. 5:9, 11:11, 33:35, 35:7, 48:29, 49:3, 67:12). Unbelievers' only chance is if they "repent and make amends" (2:160, 3:89, 4:16, 146; 5:39, 24:5).

Another pseudo-aphoristic formula acknowledges that the deity has power over both life and death. "Allah gives you life and then causes you to die" (2:28, 258; 3:156, 7:158, 9:116, 10:56, 15:23, 22:66, 23:80, 26:81, 40:68, 44:8, 45:26, 50:43, 57:2). Allah can also "bring forth the living from the dead and the dead from the living" (3:27, 6:95, 10:31, 30:19), a clear reference to resurrection. Since Allah controls death, He forbids the taking of another person's life as proclaimed in an amplification of one of the Ten Commandments, namely, "Thou Shalt Not Kill." The formulaic version in the *Qur'an* is "Slay not the soul—which Allah has forbidden—except in the course of justice" (6:151, 17:33, 25:68).

Death is clearly inevitable: "Every soul shall taste of death" (3:185, 21:35, 29:57), but on the other hand, there is the question of the possibility of life after death. "Does Allah promise that when you are dead and become dust and bones that you will be raised to life again?" (23:35, 82; 37:16, 53; 50:3, 56:47). For those who accept Allah's guidance, "No fear shall be on them, neither shall they sorrow" (2:38, 62, 112, 262, 274, 277; 3:170, 5:69, 6:48, 7:35, 49; 10:62, 41:30, 43:68, 46:13). Heaven is reserved for "those who believe and do good deeds" (2:25, 82, 277; 3:57, 4:57, 122, 173; 5:9, 93; 7:42, 10:4, 9; 11:23, 13:29, 14:23, 18:30, 107; 19:60, 96; 22:14, 23, 50, 56; 24:55, 26:227, 29:7, 9, 58; 30:15, 45; 31:8, 32:19, 34:4, 35:7, 38:24, 28; 40:58, 41:8, 42:22, 26; 45:21, 30; 47:2, 12; 48:29, 65:11, 84:25, 85:11, 95:6, 98:7, and 103:3). In heaven, there are various pleasures that await the believers—specifically the male believers—namely, the wide-eyed *houris* (44:54, 52:20, cf. 38:52, 55:72), young maidens, demure in demeanor, modestly avoiding eye contact, "restraining their glances" (37:48, 38:52, 55:56), whose virginity is attested by means of striking similes. They are as chaste as "pearls hidden in their shells" (56:23, cf. 52:24, 76:19) or as the "hidden eggs of ostriches" (37:49), "untouched by man or jinn" (55:56, 74). The general formula used to convey chastity seems to be "women who guard their private parts" (23:5, 24:31, 70:29, cf. 33:35). According to one folk belief, each (male) believer will be assigned forty *houris* in paradise (Stephan 1928:215). Once having been admitted to paradise, one is safe for eternity, able "to abide therein forever" (4:57, 122, 169; 5:119, 9:22, 100; 18:3, 33:65, 64:9, 65:11, 98:8, cf. 72:23).

There are also other formulas describing heaven and hell. In heaven, for example, we find "gardens beneath which rivers flow" (2:25, 3:15, 136, 195, 198; 4:13, 57, 122; 5:12, 85, 119; 9:72, 89, 100; 10:9, 13:35, 14:23, 16:31, 18:31, 20:76, 22:14, 23; 25:10, 47:12, 48:5, 17; 57:12, 58:22, 61:12, 64:9, 65:11, 66:8, 85:11, 98:8). The more than thirty instances of this formula, sometimes rendered in translation as "gardens watered by running streams," make it one of the more popular commonplaces. In only about one-third of the cases are the gardens in question specifically referred to as the "Gardens of Eden" (9:72, 13:23, 16:31, 18:31, 19:61, 20:76, 35:33, 38:50, 40:8, 61:12, 98:8). Sometimes the celestial scene is described as consisting of "gardens and fountains" (26:134, 147; 44:25, 52; 51:15). Ideal gardens on earth are described as

Folklore in the *Qur'an* 45

containing "date palms and grape vines" (2:266, 16:11, 17:91, 23:19, 36:34). Of course, it makes perfect sense for a population dwelling in a dry desert to perceive heaven as containing an abundance of running water (Haleem 2001:29–41). In many of these instances, there is a formula that follows celebrating the arrival of the believers in the gardens: "That is the supreme triumph" (4:13, 5:119, 9:72, 89, 100; 44:57, 48:5, 57:12, 61:12, 64:9, 85:11). On the other hand, this latter formula is encountered in other contexts not specifically referring to the gardens of paradise (9:111, 10:64, 37:60, 40:9, 45:30).

The cool waters of heaven are contrasted with the hot fires of hell wherein the unbelievers are "roasted" (4:115, 14:29, 38:56). They will be told, "Taste ye the torment of the burning" (3:181, 8:50, 22:22) or "the fire" (32:20, 34:42, cf. 22:9, 34:12). For unbelievers, "their abode is the fire" (3:151, 5:72, 10:8, 24:57, 29:25, 32:20, 45:34, 57:15) or "their refuge shall be Gehenna" (3:162, 197; 4:97, 121; 8:16, 9:73, 95; 13:18, 17:97, 66:9). Sometimes "Gehenna" or "Fire" is followed by a brief evaluative formula: "an evil destination (resting place)" (3:162, 197; 4:97, 8:16, 9:73, 13:18, 22:72, 24:57, 48:6, 57:15, 58:8, 64:10, 66:9, 67:6). The unbelievers shall be "the inmates of the Fire, in it they shall abide forever" (2:39, 81, 217, 257, 275; 3:116, 7:36, 10:27, 13:5, 58:17, 64:10). For unbelievers, "there awaits them a painful chastisement" (2:10, 104, 174, 178; 3:77, 91, 177, 188; 4:138, 5:36, 94; 9:61, 79; 14:22, 16:63, 104, 117; 24:19, 29:23, 42:21, 42; 45:11, 58:4, 59:15, 64:5). Part of the punishment of the unbelievers involves the imposition of "chains round their necks" (13:5, 34:33, 36:8, 40:71, 76:4), or being "bound together with chains" (14:49, 25:13, 38:38). There are many reminders of the consequences of leading a sinful life: "Consider the fate of the evildoers" (7:86, 103, 27:14, 28:40). "Evil-doers shall have no one to help them" (2:270, 3:192, 5:72, 22:71, 35:37, 42:8).

Because of the variety of voices in the *Qur'an* (Dashti 1985:149; Sells 1999:20)—sometimes Allah speaks to Muhammad, sometimes Muhammad speaks to Allah or perhaps to his audience of listeners, sometimes Muhammad refers to Allah in the third person, and so on— the oral formulas have had to be flexible enough to accommodate such alternation. In the third surah, we have "**Our Lord**, forgive **Thou** our sins and acquit us of our evil deeds" (3:193). In the fourth surah, "**We** will acquit **you** of your evil deeds" (4:31). In the fifth surah, "**I** will acquit **you** of your evil deeds" (5:12). In the forty-seventh surah, "**He** will acquit **them** of their evil deeds" (47:2), and in the sixty-fourth surah, "**Allah** will acquit **him** of his evil deeds" (64:9). The basic formula remains intact regardless of the nominal identity of the agent and the shift in pronouns.

We can easily see the same pronominal flexibility in such formulas as "it is no sin for **you**" (2:198, 233, 234, 240, 282; 4:23, 24, 101, 102; 24:29, 61; 33:5), "it is no sin for **them**" (2:229, 230, 233; 4:128, 24:60), and "it is no sin for **him**" (2:158). There are also the following variations: "Our signs are recited to **them**" (8:31, 10:15, 19:73, 22:72, 34:43, 45:25), "Our signs are recited to **him**" (68:15, 83:13), and "My signs were recited to **you**" (23:66, 105).

Another example of variation in a formula is provided by Allah's promise that whosoever follows His guidance, "No fear shall come upon them, nor shall they grieve" (2:38, 62, 112, 262, 277, 3:170, 5:69, 6:48, 7:35, 46:13). But there is also "you shall have no fear, nor shall you grieve" (7:49), "do not fear nor grieve" (28:7), "fear not, nor grieve" (29:33), "fear not nor be grieved" (41:30), "there is no fear for you this day, nor shall you grieve" (43:68). The challenge of translation notwithstanding, there can be no question that these are essentially all slightly altered versions of a single formula.

Dramatic pronominal shifts can be noted in the various renderings of the formula describing how Allah puts believers on the "straight path." "**He** guides **whomsoever** He will to a straight path" (2:142, 213; 3:101, 6:39, 10:25, 24:46). There is also "**He** guides **them** to a straight path" (5:16); "**You** will surely guide **them** to a straight path" (42:52); "**We** guided **them** to a straight path" (6:87); "**My Lord** has guided **me** to a straight path" (6:161); "May **Allah** ... guide **thee** on a straight path" (48:2); "**Allah** surely guides **those who believe** to a straight path" (22:54); "Guide **us** to the straight path" (1:6, cf. 38:22).

Similarly, we find "Glory be to **Allah**" (12:108, 21:22, 23:91, 27:8, 28:68, 30:17, 37:159, 52:43, 59:23, 68:29), and "Glory be to **Him**"

(2:116, 4:171, 6:100, 9:31, 10:18, 68; 16:1, 57; 17:1, 43; 19:35, 21:26, 30:40, 36:36, 83; 39:4, 67; 43:13), and "Glory be to **thee**" (2:32, 3:191, 7:143, 10:10, 21:87, 24:16, 25:18, 34:41), and finally, "Glory be to my (our, your) **Lord**" (17:93, 108; 37:180, 43:82).

Another illustration is provided by the formula whose most common wording is "There is no god but **He**" (2:163, 255; 3:2, 6, 18; 4:87, 6:106, 7:158, 9:31, 129; 10:90, 11:14, 13:30, 20:8, 23:116, 27:26, 28:70, 88; 35:3, 39:6, 40:3, 62, 65; 44:8, 59:22, 23; 64:13, 73:9). But we also find, although much less often, "There is no god but **I**" (20:14, 21:25) and "There is no god but **Thou**" (21:87). Such dramatic shifts in pronouns as well as addressees have long been noted by students of the *Qur'an*, but never with respect to their occurrence in oral formulas. (For an enlightening and persuasive detailed argument that such grammatical shifts are a traditional aspect of Arabic rhetorical style, see Haleem 1992, 2001:184–210.) Sometimes the formula "There is no god but Him" is followed by another formula, "How then can you turn away?" (35:3, 40:62, cf. 6:95, 29:61, 43:87).

If we keep in mind that the fundamental identifying hallmark characteristics of folklore are (1) multiple existence, and (2) variation, then the existence of slight variation occurring among different instances of a given formula should come as no surprise. For example, consider one of the formulas utilized in describing what will happen to those individuals fortunate enough to arrive in heaven. "They shall be decked with bracelets of gold, and arrayed in garments of fine green silk and rich brocade" (18:31); "They shall be decked with bracelets of gold and of pearls, and arrayed in garments of silk" (22:23); "They shall be decked with bracelets of gold and pearls, and arrayed in robes of silk" (35:33); and "They shall be arrayed in garments of fine green silk and rich brocade, and adorned with bracelets of silver" (76:21). From a folkloristic perspective, there is absolutely no doubt that we have four versions of one and the same oral formula.

One formula invites listeners to "Roam the earth and see what was the fate of those that disbelieved" (3:137, 6:11, 16:36, 27:69, 30:42), while a slight alteration of the formula changes the imperative to a rhetorical question: "Have they not traveled the land and seen what was the end of those who disbelieved before them?" (12:109, 30:9, 35:44, 40:21, 82; 47:10). In like fashion, the imperative "Give Allah a generous loan" (5:12, 73:20; cf. 57:18, 64:17) can be transformed into "Who will give a generous loan to Allah?" (2:245, 57:11). A comparable formulaic transformation features the shift from the declarative "Allah created the heavens and the earth" to the interrogative "'Who created the heavens and the earth?' they will say Allah" (29:61, 31:25, 39:38, 43:9). It is probably worth noting that there are patterns of rhetorical formulas cast in question form. One example is "And what shall teach thee what is _____?" (69:3, 74:27, 77:14, 82:17, 18; 83:8, 19; 86:2, 90:12, 97:2, 101:3, 10; 104:5). The blank slot can be filled with a variety of topics ranging from the "Day of Doom" (82:17, 18) to the "Night of Power" (97:2).

Another formula warns unbelievers who worship idols that "the deities they invented will forsake them" (6:24, 7:53, 10:30, 11:21, 16:87, 28:75), but there is a variant occurring in the form of a doomsday question and answer: "'Where are your idols now that you called upon besides Allah?' They will answer, 'They have forsaken us'" (7:37, 40:73). There is another version of the same taunt also addressed by Allah to unbelievers on the Day of Judgment: "On that day, He will call to them, saying, 'Where are the gods you imagined were My partners?'" (28:62, 74; 41:47).

There is one formula that specifically contrasts Allah with the rival pagan idols: "Exalted be Allah above their idols" (7:190, 10:18, 16:1, 3; 23:92, 27:63, 28:68, 30:40, 39:67).

Sometimes the formulaic variation consists of little more than the presence or absence of a single phrase. For instance, "Your Lord is Allah who created the heavens and the earth in six days and then ascended the throne" (7:54, 10:3, 11:7, 57:4) can also be found as "It was Allah who in six days created the heavens and the earth *and all that lies between them*, and then ascended the throne" (25:59, 32:4). In other versions, it is the phrases *in six days* and *ascended the throne* that are absent: "We created the heavens and earth and all that lies between them" (15:85, 30:8, 38:27, 44:38, 46:3, 50:38), or "He is the Lord of the heavens and the earth and all that lies between them" (19:65, 37:5, 38:66, 43:85, 44:7, 78:37). As for the reference to a physical throne, Allah is often described as the "Lord of the (glorious) throne" (9:129, 17:42, 23:86, 116; 27:26, 43:82, 81:20, 85:15).

Other times, the variation involves more substantial alternative wordings. Thus one way of Allah's indicating his unwillingness to allow unbelievers to hear and understand the *Qur'an* is: "We have cast veils over their hearts lest they understand Our words, and made them hard of hearing" (6:25, 17:46, 18:57, cf. 41:4). Another version of the same formula: "Allah has set a seal upon their hearts and their hearing" (2:7, cf. 4:155, 7:101, 9:87, 93; 16:108, 30:59, 40:35, 47:16, 63:3). One of the things that happens when individuals fall away from the true faith is that their "hearts become hardened" (2:74, 5:13, 6:43, 10:88, 39:22, 57:16) so that they forget Allah and are instead inclined toward Satan.

Another example of minor variation may be observed in what is very likely a proverb: "Eat and drink to your heart's content. This is the reward of your labors" (52:19). This may be compared to "Therefore eat and drink and rejoice" (19:26) and "Eat and drink to your heart's content: your recompense for what you did in days gone by" (69:24) and "Eat and drink joyously because of what you did" (77:43). Similar variation can be observed in what is apparently the same proverb in the Old and New Testaments (Dundes 1999:78–79). There are five versions alone in Ecclesiastes, one of which is "Every man should eat and drink, and enjoy the good of all his labor" (3:13).

In a few instances, the variation is so extreme that it is not entirely certain that the identical formula is involved. For example, the day of doom is marked by the "heavens cracking, the earth split asunder, and the mountains crumbling to dust" (19:90) but also is described as "when the earth shakes and quivers, and the mountains crumble away and scatter abroad into fine dust" (56:5). Still, it is probable, if not likely, that we do indeed have two versions of a standard formula, especially in the light of other passages such as "the earth with all its mountains is raised high and with one mighty crash is flattened into dust . . . the sky will be rent asunder on that day" (69:14, cf. 89:21), and "on the day when the earth shall quiver with all its mountains, and the mountains crumble into heaps of shifting sand" (73:14). These mountains, by the way, are presumably the same ones that Allah originally created as part of terra firma, ensuring that while men might shake, the earth would stay in place. "He set firm mountains upon the earth, lest it shake with you" (16:15, 21:31, 31:10), the "immovable mountains" (15:19, 50:7) serving to "make the earth a fixed place" (27:61, 40:64).

In a way, the formulaic nature of the *Qur'an* is signaled by the fact that with one single exception, surah 9, every one of the one hundred and fourteen surahs begins with the same prefatory invocational formula, the *bismillah*, (transliterated variously, e.g., "basmalah"), consisting of "In the Name of Allah, the Compassionate, the Merciful." This formula is so obvious that even scholars with little interest in or knowledge of oral-formulaic theory have commented on it. It is found only once in the *Qur'an* outside of its introductory position in one hundred and thirteen surahs, and that is in the twenty-seventh surah. What is of interest here is that it comes at the very beginning of a message from Solomon to the Queen of Sheba. She reads the message to her nobles in attendance and it is clear from the context that "In the name of Allah, the Compassionate, the Merciful" (27:30) is functioning as an opening formula for the message/letter, in effect, mimicking the same function for the *Qur'an* in general. This key formula has become part and parcel of everyday Muslim life as it ritually "precedes countless daily acts such as drinking or eating" (Graham 2001:39) or "on leaving the house in the morning or returning to it before sleeping" (Haleem 2001:28). We may conclude, therefore, that in quotidian ritual, just as in the text of the *Qur'an* itself, the formula would appear to have a remarkably consistent apotropaic aspect.

The ubiquitous presence of the *Qur'an* in everyday life in the Islamic world is difficult to convey. In Tehran, for example, one can punch buttons one, one, four (114) on a push-button telephone in order to listen to one's choice of the one hundred fourteen surahs of the *Qur'an* (Chodkiewicz 2001:28). Respect for the physical form of the *Qur'an* is demonstrated by the fact that "It is never placed on the floor or under books or objects, nor is it allowed to touch the feet or shoes or to get dirty" (al Faruqi 1987a:6). Some believers in Iran kiss the *Qur'an* when taking it into their hands in order to show proper respect (Donaldson 1937:254). Since no one may touch the *Qur'an* "except the purified" (56:380), it is understandable that individuals perform the requisite ceremonial ablutions before doing so (Donaldson 1937:254).

Less common as an opening formula is a series of words for letters in the Arabic alphabet: "Alif Lam Mim" (2:1, 3:1, 29:1, 30:1, 31:1, 32:1), "Alif Lam Ra" (10:1, 11:1, 12:1, 14:1, 15:1), "Alif Lam Mim Ra" (13:1), and "Alif Lam Mim Sad" (7:1). (Another such opening formula is "Ha Mim" [40:1, 41:1, 42:1, 43:1, 44:1, 45:1, 46:1].) Much ink has been spilled attempting to decipher the possible meaning or significance of these likely acronymic formulas. One possible theory suggests that they are abbreviations of the more common *basmallah* (Bellamy 1973) although, to be sure, they do not occur in place of the *basmallah* but rather in addition to it as a second opening formula.

What has not been noticed is the stylistic fact that within a given surah, a large majority of the verses all end with a formula. In effect, the formula functions as a kind of oral literary coda. In a few instances, the same closing formula is used for each verse in a surah. For example, in surah 55, the formula "O which then of your Lord's blessings would you [plural: men and jinn] deny?" is repeated thirty-one times. (This formula appears in just one other surah [53:55].) In surah 77, a refrain-like formula is repeated ten times, apparently at the conclusion of verses: "Woe on that day to those [disbelievers] who reject the truth" (77:15, 19, 24, 28, 34, 37, 40, 45, 47, 49), and it is found in just two other surahs (52:11, 83:10).

The fact that formulas are so often employed to signal the end of a verse can serve as a helpful means to facilitate the very identification of formulas. So if a given phrase recurs and specifically if it recurs at the conclusion of various verses, this would appear to confirm that it is indeed a formula. Accordingly, when we find "Allah knows and you do not" at the end of verse 2:216, we cannot really be certain of its formulaic status. But when we also find it at the end of 2:232, 3:66, and 24:19, we may more readily and reasonably speculate that it is truly a formula. In the same way, we can see that praise for Allah's judging skills is summarized at the end of verse 7:87 as "He is the best of judges." By itself, this proves nothing, but then we find the same phrase at the end of verse 12:80. Even more persuasive is the occurrence of the identical phrase at the end of 10:109 that is also the concluding element of the entire tenth surah. There seems little doubt that "He is the best of judges" is one of the many formulas in the *Qur'an*.

The same logic prevails in the case of the phrase, "Evil is the abode of the arrogant." We find it at the end of a verse in the sixteenth surah (16:29), at the end of a verse in the thirty-ninth surah (39:72), and once more at the end of a verse in the fortieth surah (40:76). This would appear to be another example of a formula functioning as a kind of literary coda. The same holds for the charge that unbelievers lie: "Surely they are liars" (6:28, 16:86, 29:12, 37:152, 58:18).

The overwhelming formulaic composition of the *Qur'an* is also attested by the fact that whole verses consist of little else than formulas. Several representative examples standing for many should suffice. In surah 39, the seventh verse includes: "No soul shall bear another's burden. To your Lord shall you return and He will declare to you what you have done. He knows your innermost thoughts." As already noted, "No soul shall bear another's burden" is a formula; "To your Lord shall you return" is a formula" (3:83, 5:48, 105; 6:60, 108, 164; 7:125, 10:4, 11:4, 34; 19:40, 26:50, 28:88, 29:8, 17; 30:11, 31:15, 23; 32:11, 36:22, 39:7, 44; 40:43, 41:21, 42:15, 43:14, 85; 45:15), and so is "He will declare to you what you have done" (5:105, 6:60, 108, 159; 9:94, 105; 24:64, 39:7, 58:6, 7; 62:8), as well as "He knows your innermost thoughts." The verse thus consists entirely of a sequence of individual distinctive oral formulas.

Consider the fourth verse of surah 57. "To Allah belongs the kingdom of the heavens and the earth. To Allah shall all things return. He causes the night to pass into the day and causes the day to pass into the night. He has knowledge of the innermost thoughts of men." The first line is an oft-repeated standard formula (2:107, 255, 284; 3:109, 129, 189; 4:126, 131, 132, 170, 171; 5:17, 18, 40, 120; 7:158, 10:55, 68; 14:2,

16:52, 20:6, 21:19, 24:42, 64; 30:26, 31:26, 42:4, 49; 45:27, 48:14, 57:2, 5). The second line, "To Allah shall all things return," is also a standard formula (2:210, 3:109, 8:44, 11:123, 22:76, 35:4, 57:5). The next two lines are also separate formulas. Once again, we have a sequential series of formulas. These are by no means unique instances. We find throughout the *Qur'an* formula piled upon formula in surah after surah.

In attempting to understand the endless agglomeration of repeated formulas in the *Qur'an*, one must keep in mind that such repetition is one of the very hallmarks of oral tradition. One of the most prominent of Danish folklorist Axel Olrik's famous "epic laws of folk narrative" was "Das Gesetz der Wiederholung" (the law of repetition), and Arabic oral tradition is no exception. The important role of repetition in the *Arabian Nights*, for example, has been well documented (Naddaff 1991), and it has been suggested, in any event, that Muhammad approved of repetition (Glubb 1979:135).

There is a recurring oral formula that is one of several phrases that impugn the very truth-value of the *Qur'an*. The critical formulas suggesting that Muhammad may be telling outright fabricated lies are invariably put in the mouths of the unbelievers, the disbelievers, the skeptics, the very same individuals who insisted that Muhammad's revelations were nothing but "an invented falsehood," claiming "this is nothing but (manifest) sorcery" (5:110, 6:7, 10:76, 11:7, 27:13, 28:36, 34:43, 37:15, 46:7, 61:6, 74:24). Interestingly enough, it is the unbelievers who in turn are accused by Muhammad of relying upon unsubstantiated speculation instead of accepting Allah's revelations. The most telling formula is "They [unbelievers] follow nothing but mere conjecture" (4:157, 6:116, 148; 10:36, 66; 53:23, 28), and this formula is usually followed by either "They do nothing but lie" (6:116, 148; 10:66) or "Conjecture is no substitute for the truth" (10:36, 53:28). Even so, the same basic charge is leveled at Muhammad, and it is this formula that has provided the title of the present extended essay.

The version of the verse in surah 6:25 is typical: "When they come to argue with you, the unbelievers say: 'This is nothing but fables of the ancients.'" Surah 8:31 repeats the formula: "Whenever Our revelations are recited to them, they say: 'We have heard them. If we wished, we could say the like. They are but fables of the ancients.'" The very same formula is found in a reference to Judgment Day: "On that day woe betide the disbelievers who deny the Last Judgement! None denies it except the evil transgressor who, when Our revelations are recited to him, cries: 'Fables of the ancients!'" (83:13; cf. 16:24, 23:83, 25:5, 27:68, 46:17, 68:15). Still another formula found in the *Qur'an* confirming the negative connotation of folk narratives refers to earlier unsuccessful attempts by emissaries from the deity to enlighten the people: "And we reduced them to so many tales and legends" (23:44, 34:19) as translated by Mir (1989:77). Is there any validity whatsoever to the formulaic taunt repeatedly addressed to Muhammad? Are there indeed any "fables of the ancients" in the *Qur'an*?

FOLKTALES IN THE *QUR'AN*

Ever since the publication of Finnish folklorist Antti Aarne's (1867–1925) *Verzeichnis der Märchentypen* in 1910 as the third monograph in the prestigious Folklore Fellows Communications series, folklorists have been accustomed to identifying international folktales by an agreed-upon convention of assigned tale type numbers. Twice revised by American folklorist Stith Thompson (1885–1976), in 1928 and in 1961, the Aarne-Thompson tale type index has provided a convenient and ready means of referring to folktales. In this system, for example, the tale commonly known in English as "Cinderella" is Aarne-Thompson tale type 510A; "Little Red Riding Hood" is Aarne-Thompson tale type 333. There are approximately 2,000 such Indo-European and Semitic tale types listed in the 1961 revision of the index.

With the help of the Aarne-Thompson tale type index, we can distinguish at least three distinct tale types in the *Qur'an*, although they are not identified as such by the entry on the *Qur'an* in the authoritative *Enzyklopädie des Märchens* (Nagel 1994). Undoubtedly, one reason why Islamic scholars have been reluctant to acknowledge the presence of identifiable tale types in the *Qur'an* has to do with one of the distinguishing characteristics of the folktale genre. Folktales, as opposed to other genres of folk narrative such as myth and legend, are clearly regarded as fiction. The typical opening formulas, "Once upon a time," "Es war einmal," "Il était une fois," "Érase una vez," signal to the audience that the narrative that follows is to be regarded as fictional, not factual in the historic sense. No listener believes that there was a historical young girl named Cinderella or one named Little Red Riding Hood. In the context of assuming that the *Qur'an* is God's truth as revealed by the angel Gabriel to Muhammad, it should be obvious why there would be resistance to calling attention to the existence of tale types in the *Qur'an*.

The first of the tale types to be discussed is Aarne-Thompson tale type 766, "The Seven Sleepers." The succinct summary in the tale type index states: "Magic sleep extending over many years." The version in the *Qur'an* is contained in surah 18, "The Cave." The plot involves seven young men who were believers. To escape death at the hands of pagan unbelievers, they sought refuge in a cave. There they fell asleep "while their dog lay at the cave's entrance with legs outstretched" (18:18). Eventually they awoke, wondering how long they had been there. "A day, or less than a day" was one guess (18:19). It was decided that one of the group should venture into the city to bring back food. He was urged to be careful lest they be captured and forced to renounce their faith in favor of the pagan ways of unbelievers. But their secret was revealed and the seven soon thereafter died in the cave. The people who discovered the bodies built a place of worship over these martyrs. Then the account in the *Qur'an* indulges in a bit of purely folkloristic discussion concerning the number of sleepers involved: "Some will say: 'The sleepers were three: their dog was the fourth.' Others, guessing at the unknown, will say: 'They were five: their dog was the sixth.' And yet others: 'Seven: their dog was the eighth'" (18:23). The narrative voice, functioning as a folklorist, seems well aware that there are different versions of the tale. And as any good folklorist might say, even today, there is really no way of knowing which version, if any, is the correct one. "Say: 'My Lord best knows their number.'" In other words, God knows which version is correct, but no one else does. Even the duration of the time spent in the cave is subject to variation in different versions. "Some say they stayed in the cave three hundred years, and (some) add nine more. Say: 'None but God knows how long they stayed in it'" (18:26).

The tale is typically interpreted in Islamic as well as Christian tradition as an allegorical expression of the "reality of bodily resurrection" (Heller 1904:215; Brown 1983:165; Roberts 1993:316). In the *Qur'an*, Allah's power to resurrect believers is articulated in formulaic fashion: "He originates creation, then He brings it back again" (10:4, 34; 21:104, 27:64, 29:19, 30:11, 27; 85:13). "He will surely gather you all together on the Day of Resurrection: that day is not to be doubted" (3:9, 4:87, 6:12, 45:26). "Be mindful of your duty to Allah and remember that you shall all be gathered before Him in the end" (2:203, 5:96, 6:72, 58:9). Unbelievers are skeptical about the eschatological premise of resurrection, considering it a false promise. "There is only the life in this world. We live and we die" (23:37, 45:24, cf. 6:29). But Allah's ability to resuscitate the dead is explicit in the frequent formulaic reference to His sending abundant water from the sky (6:6, 11:52, 71:11, cf. 2:22, 164; 6:99, 13:17, 16:10, 65; 18:45, 23:18, 25:48, 30:24, 31:10, 35:27, 39:21, 50:9), by which means "He revives the earth after its death" (2:164, 7:57, 16:65, 22:5, 25:49, 29:63, 30:19, 24, 50; 35:9, 36:33, 41:39, 43:11, 45:5, 50:11, 57:17). "We send down water upon it, it stirs and swells" (22:5, 41:39).

In the tale, the youths are asleep for three hundred years, seemingly dead, but are then miraculously brought to life after that long period of time. Elsewhere in the *Qur'an*, in descriptions of the Day of Judgment, time spent in the grave seems to those who have been resurrected as having been no more than an hour or less than a day. "The day will come when Allah will gather them all together as though they had tarried but for an hour" (10:45, 30:55, 46:35). "And He will ask, 'How many years did you linger on the earth?' They will reply: 'A day, or less than a day'" (23:113, cf. 79:46). In Stith Thompson's *Motif-Index of Folk-Literature*, this is Motif D2011. Years thought days. However, such a supernatural lapse of time is typically found in connection with sojourns in fairyland (cf. Hartland 1890:161–254). The striking contrast between perceptions of the duration of divine and earthly time is alluded to in the formula, "A day with Allah is like a thousand years in your reckoning" (22:47, 32:5, cf. 97:3), a formula that may be cognate with, "For a thousand years in thy sight are but as yesterday when it is past" found in the Psalms (90:4).

The supernatural lapse of time motif is encountered elsewhere in the *Qur'an*. In the second surah, we are told of a man who when passing a city in ruins asked, "How can Allah give life to this city, now that it is dead?" Whereupon Allah caused the man to die and after one hundred years brought him back to life. Allah then asked him, "How long have you tarried?" "A day or less than a day," the man replied. "No," said Allah, "You were dead a hundred years. Just look at your food and drink; they are not spoiled and look at your ass. For we will make you a sign for mankind. Look at the bones, how we scatter them and then clothe them with flesh." When the man understood this, he said, "I know that Allah has power over all things" (2:259). As in the case of the tale of the seven sleepers, the motif serves as an allegory for resurrection. The repetition of the formula "A day or less than a day" (2:259, 18:19, cf. 23:113) even links the two narratives (Hartland 1890:182).

There have been scores and scores of discussions of the tale of the seven sleepers, but most are written by nonfolklorists who label it a "parable" (Gluck 1982:76; Roberts 1993). A representative sampling of the abundant scholarship would include John Koch 1883; Bernhard Heller 1904; P. Michael Huber 1910; Wilhelm Weyh 1911; Paul Sartori 1935–1936; Ignazio Guidi 1945; Ernest Honigmann 1953; Louis Massignon 1969:3:104–118; François Jourdan 1983; and Norman O. Brown 1983. One of the most massive documentations of the tale was a collaborative effort by several scholars in a series of reports entitled "Les Sept Dormants d'Éphèse en Islam et en Chrétienté," published in the *Revue des Études Islamiques*. Appropriately enough, there are seven parts, accompanied by forty plates. The series includes references to texts, sites associated with the seven sleepers, and numerous illustrations taken from murals and stained glass windows depicting the sleepers in a cave (Dermenghem et al. 1954–1961, cf. Moubarac 1961 and Massignon 1969, 3:119–80). Nevertheless, to my knowledge, no one has previously recognized the narrative as an international tale type as such. Admittedly, one could certainly take issue with Thompson's decision to classify the narrative as a tale type that would per se indicate that the story was to be defined as a folktale. Inasmuch as the story is more often than not told as true, as a purported historical happening, it might be more appropriate to classify it as "migratory legend" (Bødker 1965:198–99). All narratives classified as legends share the characteristic of being told as true (as opposed to folktales, which are typically told as fiction). Similarly, the account of the Wandering Jew who is doomed to wander endlessly, unable to die, as a punishment for blasphemy, which Thompson classified as tale type 777, would also appear to be a migratory legend. The generic confusion about "The Seven Sleepers" is not new. The brothers Grimm, for example, included "Die sieben Schlafenden Männer in der höhle" [The seven sleeping men in the cave] as legend 392 in their collection of German legends (1865, 2:27–28), but a similar story, "The Twelve Apostles," is contained as tale 202 in their more famous collection of folktales (1987:637). The question of genre is not purely academic inasmuch as there are obvious ramifications of generic distinctions. Legends, for example, are almost always told as true and in many instances, including legends related about saints or other historic personages, there is often the presumption of historicity or at least the possibility of a kernel of truth. In contrast, as already mentioned, folktales are purely fictional. In this case, a **legend** found in the *Qur'an* has in theory the chance if not likelihood of containing an element of historical truth, whereas a **folktale** would not. Nonetheless, whether "The Seven Sleepers" story is a folktale or a migratory legend (cf. Lüthi 1976:35–46), the fact remains that it clearly belongs to the realm of folklore, and furthermore there seem to be Christian versions that antedate the version in the *Qur'an*.

Finally, there is a telltale clue pointing to the veritable certainty that the *Qur'an* version of "The Seven Sleepers" was borrowed from an earlier source and that is the presence of the dog. Dogs are deemed to be impure in the Moslem world (Lévy 1934: 581) and it is undoubtedly only the tenacity of tradition that can account for the otherwise inexplicable retention of this element of the story in a section of the most sacred book of Islam.

A second tale type is found in the same surah. Moses is accompanied by a mysterious servant who performs strange acts that puzzle Moses. The servant has previously warned Moses that there would be actions beyond his understanding. The servant says, "If you are bent on following me, you must not question me about anything until I mention it to you myself." Moses agrees. The two then board a ship but Moses' companion proceeds to bore a hole in the bottom of the ship. Moses momentarily forgets his pledge and asks if his companion meant to drown the ship's passengers. The companion chastises Moses for questioning him and Moses apologizes. The two continue their journey and are joined by a certain youth who is then slain by the servant. Again Moses violates his pledge and asks why an innocent youth was killed. And again the servant scolds Moses for questioning his action and again Moses apologizes. Finally, the two come to a city where they ask for food at a house where there is a wall in disrepair. The servant restores the wall, whereupon Moses claims that he could have asked the owners of the house for payment for his labor.

At this point, the servant parts from Moses but before doing so explains the three strange actions.

> Know that the ship belonged to some poor fishermen. I damaged it because at their rear there was a king who was taking every ship by force. As for the youth, his parents both are true believers, and we feared lest he should plague them with wickedness and unbelief. It was our wish that their Lord should grant them another in his place, a son more righteous and more filial. As for the wall, it belonged to two orphan boys in the city whose father was an honest man. Beneath it [the wall] their treasure is buried. Your Lord decreed, as a mercy from your Lord, that they should dig up their treasure when

they grow to manhood. What I did was not done by my will. That
is the meaning of what you could not bear to watch with patience.
(18:70–84)

This is unquestionably a version of Aarne-Thompson tale type 759, "God's Justice Vindicated" (The Angel and the Hermit). The tale type summary reads: "An angel takes a hermit with him and does many seemingly unjust things (repays hospitality by stealing a cup; inhospitality by giving a cup; hospitality by throwing his host's servant from a bridge and by killing the host's son. The angel shows the hermit why each of these was just." Fortunately, the relationship of the *Qur'an*ic narrative to the tale type has been exhaustively discussed by Haim Schwarzbaum in his erudite 1959 essay, "Jewish and Moslem Versions of Some Theodicy Legends," leaving absolutely no doubt of its cognate status. Other studies of this tale type include those by Gaston Paris (1881), Israel Lévi (1884), Anton Schönbach (1901), and the unpublished doctoral dissertation of Heinz-Wilhelm Haase (1966).

Perhaps the most famous literary version of the tale was written by Françoise-Marie Arouet (1694–1778), who during a period of imprisonment in the Bastille in 1717–1718 changed his name to Voltaire. In his 1747 work *Zadig or Destiny: An Oriental Tale*, the title character Zadig has a series of adventures or misadventures. In the chapter entitled "The Hermit," Zadig encounters a white-bearded hermit who agrees to travel with him provided that Zadig promises not to leave him for the next few days no matter what he does. The hermit then steals a gold, jewel-studded basin from hospitable hosts and then gives it to a rich miser. After another stay at a different locale, the hermit takes a torch and sets fire to the house. Finally, after a two-day sojourn at the home of a charitable widow, the hermit accompanies the widow's nephew at her request to a bridge over a raging river. The hermit picks up the boy by the hair and throws him into the water where he drowns. The hermit then explains to Zadig that under the ruins of the house set on fire, the owner has found immense treasure, and the boy who was drowned would have murdered his aunt in a year and Zadig himself in two years. The plausibility of Voltaire's source being a Jewish version of the tale is signaled by the choice of the name Zadig, which is almost certainly related to the Jewish concept of Zaddik, the righteous man (Horodezky 1913; Mach 1957; and Lichtenstein 1959).

As to whether the Jewish version of the tale type is the source for the *Qur'an*ic text, there is some question. Schwarzbaum, for example, claims that AT 759 did not appear "as a full-fledged tale type" in Jewish folk literature until the eleventh century (1959:142, n 122) and that neither a close Jewish nor a Christian parallel to the *Qur'an*ic text has yet been found (135). Wheeler in his 1998 essay also expresses doubt about a Jewish origin of the tale. That said, it is still absolutely empirically certain that the *Qur'an*ic text is indeed a version of AT 759. At the very least, the *Qur'an*ic text would provide a *terminus ante quem* for the tale type.

It is of interest that Norman O. Brown considers this particular tale as the signature plot (along with the rest of the surah) of the entire *Qur'an*. His 1983 essay, "The Apocalypse of Islam," was inspired by one written by the French Islamicist Louis Massignon, "Les 'Sept Dormants': Apocalypse de Islam" (1969, 3:104–118). Brown's reasoning is that the difference between seemingly illogical and mysterious acts and their deeper religious significance as revealed by the "angel" is emblematic of how the *Qur'an* as a whole is to be approached (Brown 1983:163). "Folktales, like dreams, are not to be interpreted literally.... The form and the content of the folktale obliges us ... to make the distinction between literal meaning and something beyond" (161). On the other hand, Brown is critical of "Western historicism, with its well-honed methods of source criticism," which he argues "is only too delighted to lose itself in tracing the *Qur'an* to its sources, with the usual nihilistic result: the *Qur'an* is reduced to a meaningless confusion" (169). But Brown exhibits some confusion himself and betrays his ignorance of folkloristics when he claims that the notion of the mysterious wise angel "is to be understood in analogy with Folktale D1960.2 in Stith Thompson's index: Barbarossa, King asleep in a mountain; will awake one day to succor his people," a plot that Brown also sees as parallel to

"The Seven Sleepers" narrative (166). D1960.2 *Kyffhäuser* is, first of all, a *motif* number in Thompson's *Motif-Index of Folk-Literature*, not a *tale type* number in the tale type index, and secondly, the story of Barbarossa is definitely a legend, not a folktale.

Now, serious scholars of the *Qur'an* have long known that "The Seven Sleepers" and "The Angel and the Hermit" were traditional tales (Nöldeke 1909:142), although they may not have realized that the two narratives were tale types in the Aarne-Thompson canon. But there is an allusion to another tale type that has not, to my knowledge, been properly identified. In surah 27, "The Ant," we find reference to a curious narrative involving a talking ant. Here is a translation of the passage:

> And Solomon was David's heir. And he said: "O men! We have been taught the language of birds, and have been given an abundance of all things. This surely is a great blessing." And there were gathered together unto Solomon his armies of the jinn and humankind, and of the birds, and they were set in battle order; Till, when they reached the Valley of the Ants, an ant exclaimed: "O ants! Enter your dwellings lest Solomon and his armies crush you, unwittingly." Solomon smiled, and laughing at her words, said: "My Lord, allow me to express my gratitude for the blessings You have bestowed on me and my parents, and the chance to do good works that shall be pleasing to Thee." (27:16–19)

Curiously, the prayer uttered by Solomon is identical to that required when a Moslem grows to manhood and attains the mature age of forty, according to another passage in the *Qur'an* (46:15).

Commentators have been puzzled by this passage, wondering about the seemingly miraculous act of an ant speaking such that it could be understood by a human. There are several clues, obvious to a trained folklorist, as to the source of this passage. First of all, we have a reference to Solomon's having "been taught the language of the birds." This immediately suggests Aarne-Thompson tale type 670, "The Animal Languages." The summary of the tale in the tale type index reads: "A man learns animal languages. His wife wants to discover his secret. The advice of the cock." The tale has been studied by Theodor Benfey (1864), James George Frazer (1888), Antti Aarne (1909, 1914), Géza Róheim (1953), and Dov Noy (1971), among others. In many versions, the protagonist is given the power to understand the language of animals on condition that he does not reveal to anyone that he can do so. He overhears the words spoken by a cock, or in some versions an ant. Amused by this, he smiles or laughs out loud, thereby arousing the curiosity of his wife who asks him what he is laughing at. Aarne notes that this element of laughing upon hearing the conversation of animals is one of the principal traits of the tale (1914:31), and it is this explicit mention of laughter in the twenty-seventh surah that has led scholars to identify the episode as one of the relatively rare occurrences of humor in the *Qur'an* (Mir 1991:181–82; for a discussion of the general lack of humor in and about the *Qur'an*, see Marzolph 2000). This particular trait of the tale is classified by folklorists as Motif N456, Enigmatic smile (laugh) reveals secret knowledge. It is also of interest that King Solomon sometimes appears in the tale (Aarne 1914:25), especially in Jewish tradition (Noy 1971:199, cf. Sidersky 1933).

One of the oldest recorded versions of the tale is a Buddhist story reported in the third century. In that version, a king rescued the daughter of a dragon-king who grants him a wish. The king says he already has many precious objects, but what he would like is to understand the language of all the animals. The dragon king grants his request, but on condition that he not reveal that he has this ability. The king, while eating with his wife, overhears a conversation between two butterflies. The female butterfly asks the male butterfly to bring her some food. He replies that everyone should serve himself. The female replies that his stomach prevents that. Hearing the exchange, the king bursts into laughter, whereupon his wife asks, "O king, why are you laughing?" (Chavannes 1910:382–83).

There is another Indic version of the tale, and one should keep in mind that the Jataka tales date from several centuries before the *Qur'an* was revealed to Muhammad. (For references to other Jataka versions of this tale type, see Grey 1990:60.) The tale is of special interest in the present context because it involves an ant. A king saves the life of the king of snakes and as a reward, the king of snakes grants him a charm "giving knowledge of all sounds." The king said, "It is well," and accepted it. "From the time he understood the voice even of ants. One day he was sitting on the dais eating solid food with honey and molasses, and a drop of honey, a drop of molasses, and morsel of cake fell on the ground. An ant seeing this comes crying, 'The king's honey jar is broken on the dais, his molasses cart and cake cart are upset. Come and eat honey and molasses and cake.' The king hearing the cry laughed. The queen being near him thought, 'What has the king seen that he laughs?'" (Cowell 1897, 3:174–77). A version even closer to the one in the *Qur'an* comes from an Annamese (Vietnamese) text. In this tale, a snake gives a man the gift of understanding the language of animals. "One day his wife went into a corner of the house where there were some ants. The ants scrambled out of her way, and the man heard them say to each other, 'Come, let us climb up to a place of safety.' He laughed. His wife wanted to know why he laughed, but he steadily refused to tell her, and she died of vexation" (Frazer 1888:171–72). As in the *Qur'an*, the ants are here trying to escape being trampled to death by humans. From these representative texts, it seems indisputable that the ant episode in the *Qur'an* is clearly an allusion to Aarne-Thompson tale type 670, "The Animal Languages."

Moreover, the popularity of this particular tale type in the Arab world is attested by its occurrence in the frame tale of *The Arabian Nights*. Shahrazad's father tells her the tale to dissuade her from accepting the challenge of marrying the king who routinely killed each new bride after just one night (Haddawy 1990:11–15).

CONCLUSION

Before discussing possible conclusions, I would like to express the hope that the findings presented in this work are not summarily dismissed

Folklore in the *Qur'an* 65

or disparaged strictly on the grounds that the writer is an orientalist-folklorist. The key questions to be taken into account include: (1) Are there oral formulas present in the *Qur'an*? and (2) Are there folktales contained in the *Qur'an*? I should think that anyone with an unbiased mind, capable of objectively evaluating empirical data, ought to be able to see that the answer to both questions is a definite resounding "yes."

Having demonstrated the presence of numerous formulas in the *Qur'an* and having identified three Aarne-Thompson tale types in the *Qur'an*, what conclusions can we draw from our findings? First of all, the long-standing claim that the *Qur'an* was orally transmitted from its very beginnings can be confirmed by the extraordinarily high percentage of formulas contained in its canonical text. While we have not provided a statistical count of the formulas with respect to the total number of lines of the *Qur'an*, it seems safe to say that the formulaic density of the *Qur'an* is well in excess of 20 percent, the supposed minimum threshold necessary to establish original orality. Indeed, it would appear likely that if one were to subtract **all** the oral formulas from the *Qur'an*, one would have an overall text reduced by as much as one-third of its present length, if not more. The high formulaic density of the *Qur'an* also suggests that Muhammad (or Allah or the archangel Gabriel) was seemingly well versed in the techniques of folkloristic oral transmission.

Even the presumed historical fact that Muhammad was forty years old (46:15) when he began to receive the *Qur'an* from Allah via Gabriel has formulaic implications. Forty is not only a ritual number in Islam (Rescher 1911), but also among all Semitic peoples (Roscher 1909) and in the Middle East generally (Rescher 1913; Hasluck 1912–1913), including both Jewish (Pinker 1994) and Christian traditions (König 1907). It continues to have ritualistic significance in the Arab world (Roscher 1909:128–29; Stephan 1928), as well as in the West—consider the word *quarantine*, which referred originally to a period of forty days' detention or isolation of a ship or its passengers upon its arrival in port because of the fear of a possible epidemic spread of a contagious disease (Roscher 1909:104). It is hardly coincidental that Moses was supposedly forty years of age when he led the children of Israel out of Egypt (Acts 7:23) and that "when forty years were expired, there appeared to him in the wilderness of Mount Sinai an angel of the Lord in a flame of fire in a bush" (Acts 7:31). Forty is not only a formula in folk narrative (Motif Z 71.12, Formulistic number: forty)—think of "Ali Baba and the Forty Thieves"—but it continues in modern times to signify a magical turning point in life: "Life begins at forty." (For discussions of Muhammad's fitting into this formulaic pattern, see Nöldeke 1909:68; Brandes 1985:68–72; and especially Conrad 1987.)

The folkloristic sophistication of Muhammad (or Allah or the archangel Gabriel) is further attested by the undeniable presence of Aarne-Thompson tale types in the *Qur'an*. Since these tale types 766, "The Seven Sleepers," 759, "The Hermit and the Angel," and 670, "The Animal Languages," surely antedate the *Qur'an*, we cannot assume that any of them were created or invented by Muhammad. This is not necessarily a problem inasmuch as one of the stylistic features of the *Qur'an* is to allude to tales *already known to the listeners* (Gluck 1982:85). Throughout the *Qur'an*, there are numerous references to events reported in both the Old and New Testaments. To the extent that these events are commented upon critically, for example, Jesus was only a mortal, a favored servant, a messenger, like Abraham, Moses, Joseph, and Muhammad himself, and *not* the son of God (2:116, 4:171, 5:17, 75; 6:101, 9:30, 10:68, 17:111, 18:4, 19:35, 88, 92; 21:26, 23:91, 25:2, 37:152, 39:4, 43:59, 81; 72:3, 112:4), the *Qur'an* would qualify not so much as history but as metahistory (Hirt 1993:53). Rarely, with the possible exception of the Potiphar's wife motif, K 2011, recounted in the twelfth surah (12:21–28), are these events recounted in full detail. One reason for this is the guiding esthetic in the *Qur'an* which, unlike that of the West, spurns linear thinking or what Olrik in his classic paper on "epic laws" refers to as "single-strandedness" in oral narrative (1999:94). Muslim critics have even charged, with some justification, that Western scholars are so imbued with a linear worldview (cf. Lee 1950) that they have sought to rearrange the order of surahs in the *Qur'an* so as to try to put the events described in some kind of chronological sequence

(Manzoor 1987:36; Serrano 2002:53). Such tampering with the order is deemed sacrilegious inasmuch as mortals, it seems, have no business altering the revealed word of Allah.

It has been suggested that the assumption that an audience was already familiar with earlier events and stories was typical of oral tradition (Lester 1999:54), but intertextuality wherein one text alludes or refers to another (earlier) one is just as common in literary practice. In any case, given the *Qur'an*'s penchant for mentioning plots from the Old and New Testaments plus oral tradition, it is not so surprising that there would be allusions to traditional tale types as well. The only troubling issue revolves around the vexing question of revelation (Saeed 1999). If the *Qur'an* is truly a divine revelation from Allah, one might well ask how something already known on earth can rightfully be said to be "revealed" by a deity.

In any event, if we keep in mind that Allah, the god of Islam, is the same monotheistic deity as that worshipped by Jews and Christians, albeit under a different name or guise, we may note that Allah or God did not hesitate to incorporate folktales in the Bible. In the Old Testament, we have Aarne-Thompson tale type 926, "Judgment of Solomon" (1 Kings 3:16–28) and in the New Testament, we have Aarne-Thompson tale type 293, "Debate of the Belly and the Members." Debate as to their usefulness. All are mutually useful (1 Corinthians 12:12–26). As folklorists, we should be very pleased and proud of the fact that our preeminent deity has such a high regard for folktales, not to mention other genres of folklore such as oaths and proverbs. Just as the *Qur'an* is believed to be the word of Allah or God, so also is the *Bible* believed to be of divine origin. "All Scripture is given by inspiration of God" (2 Timothy 3:16). There is a significant difference, however. Whereas Christians consider the New Testament to be "inspired" by God, Muslims believe the *Qur'an* to be the actual *word* of Allah (Chodkiewicz 2001:20). In any case, the presence of authentic traditional folklore in both the *Qur'an* and the Bible cannot be denied. To the oral-formulaic charge attributed to unbelievers in the *Qur'an*, so often quoted by Muhammad, that the *Qur'an* contains "ancient fables," we must say unequivocally,

"Yes, there are ancient fables in the *Qur'an*." And we might add: "What's wrong with that?" The presence of ancient fables in the *Qur'an* (and in the Bible) in no way diminishes the religious or moral value of these great sacred documents. Quite the contrary, the presence of folklore is a guarantee of their basic humanity, and, if one chooses to believe so, their divine character.

In assessing the significance of the empirically demonstrable occurrence of formulas and folktales in the *Qur'an*, it is essential that the cultural context of Arabic oral tradition be taken into account. In order to avoid the ethnocentric if not downright racist bias of the vise of orientalism—one Muslim critic has gone so far as to label orientalism as applied to the *Qur'an* "Islamophobic" (Manzoor 1987:37)—it must be kept in mind that the esthetic principles of oral tradition differ markedly from the modern standard canons of Western literary criticism. Dutch diplomat P. Marcel Kurpershoek in his comprehensive three-volume study *Oral Poetry and Narratives of Central Arabia*, based upon his own fieldwork in Saudi Arabia, states it very well: "In a traditional society like that of the Najd, the concepts of convention and originality cannot be applied in the same way as they are in the West" (1994:59). As he notes in discussing the oral tradition, "In composing, the poets make use of a common store of themes, motives, stock images, phraseology and prosodical options that together constitute the heritage of Najdi poetry" (1994:57). Saad Sowayan describes a Saudi Arabian historical oral narrative genre called *suwalif* (the singular is *salfih*) in similar terms. "Unlike a folktale or other works of fiction, the *salfih* is discursive and loosely structured with no fixed beginning or end. It usually consists of several episodes which the narrator weaves together in a clustered fashion as he goes along. He does not necessarily adhere to any predetermined order. There is no established sequence in which the episodes must follow one another. Chronological order is not always observed" (1992:22). Speaking of the narrator, Sowayan observes, "In his double role as artist and historian, an illiterate composer casts his poetic creation in a memorable form to insure its preservation in public memory. This compels him to resort to *preexisting patterns, preconceived mo-*

tifs, standard formulas, as well as other oral stylistic features and mnemonic devices" (1992:27, my emphasis). Another authority on the *salfih* genre argues along similar lines. Despite making a claim that the genre is not "susceptible . . . to any characterization as 'formulaic,'" Ingham notes that "each narrator recreates the composition and actual wording with each act of narration, although particular segments of direct speech or specific turns of phrase describing important phases of the action do recur in separate renderings," and he admits that "formulae nevertheless exist" and provides several examples (1993, 6, 18–21).

Sowayan remarks that oral poetry "is a work of art before it is a factual report of historical events. Instead of giving a detailed account of what happened, a poem only makes vague allusions and cryptic references to the events themselves" (1992:25). Although Sowayan is describing a narrative recorded in the late twentieth century referring to events that took place approximately one hundred and fifty years earlier in 1835, his, Kurpershoek's, and Ingham's comments would seem to apply very well to the *Qur'an*. From this we may speculate that the basic nature of Arabic oral tradition still to be found in the twenty-first century is very likely to be similar to that which existed in pre-Islamic times, at least with respect to the use of oral formulas and folktales.

The presence of oral formulas and folktales in the *Qur'an* is by no means incompatible with its presumed divine origin. Professor Seyyed Hossein Nasr, the first occupant of the Aga Khan Chair of Islamic Studies established at the American University of Beirut, remarked, "The formulae of the *Qur'an*, because they come from God, have a power which is not identical with what we learn from them rationally by simply reading and reciting them. They are rather like a talisman which protects and guides man" (1972:51). (For a sample of several of the traditional talismanic procedures utilizing specific passages from the *Qur'an*, see Hames 2001.)

Moreover, the documentation of the formulaic content of the *Qur'an* in this extended essay should help focus upon the central themes of this sacred text. Readers may have been put off by what they consider to be the tedious listing of occurrences of the various formulas, but these listings provide a rough quantitative indication of which themes are the most important. The simple principle would be that the more times a formula appears, the more significant the theme articulated in the formula should be regarded. Hence the diverse powers of Allah, the sharp division between believers and unbelievers, the dramatic difference between the joys of heaven and the horrors of hell, the fearsome nature of the Day of Judgment softened by the assurance of the promise of Resurrection, are all featured in numerous formulas. In theory, a reader might have gained the same appreciation of the *Qur'an*'s content by simply reading through Hanna E. Kassis's indispensable and comprehensive *vademecum*, *A Concordance of the Qur'an*, but I seriously doubt whether many would have the intestinal fortitude to read all of its 1,444 pages from cover to cover. So, aside from the demonstration of the formulaic construction of the *Qur'an*, this essay offers a relatively compact distillation of the dominant themes of this extraordinary text.

Finally, it is noteworthy that Allah Himself makes no apology for using folklore to make a point. According to a verse in surah 2, "The Cow," we are told, "Behold, God does not disdain to speak in proverbs (parables)—even that involving a gnat or a larger creature. Those who believe know that it is the truth from their Lord; those who don't believe ask 'What is it that Allah means by this proverb (parable)?' He misleads many by it and enlightens many by it. But he confounds only the sinners by it" (2:26, cf. 74:31). Similarly, in surah 14, "Abraham," we learn that "Allah speaks in parables to men so that they may take heed" (14:25) and in surah 39, "The Throngs," "We have given mankind in this *Qur'an* all manner of parables, so that they may take heed: a *Qur'an* in the Arabic tongue, free from any flaw, that they may guard themselves against evil" (39:27; cf. 18:54, 24:35, and 59:21). In surah 7, Allah, concerned with unbelievers' intractable nature with respect to tenaciously sticking to earthly desires rather than accepting His revelation, urges his followers to utilize a parable to make these reprobates think about their situation. Specifically, He mentions the parable referring to "the dog that pants if you chase it away but pants as well if you leave it alone" (7:175), presenting an image consonant with the repeated depiction of unbelievers as animals (Sabbagh 1943:248), for example, as donkeys carrying a load of books that they do not understand (62:5). There are numerous other allusions to Allah's use of parables for purposes of comparison (13:17, 16:75, 18:32, 22:73, 29:43, 47:3). The argument for the use of parables is itself evidently an oral formula! It may also be worth recalling in this context that Jesus similarly often found parables to be of great pedagogic value in his many proselytizing debates with unbelievers.

If Allah Himself acknowledges that He uses parables (which includes "folktales" in the modern sense) for the edification and enlightenment of mankind, who are we mere mortals to say otherwise or to deny the presence of folktales in the *Qur'an*? In the *Qur'an* there are indeed "fables of the ancients" placed there by divine decree, full of worldly wisdom to be favored and savored for generations to come.

Bibliography

Aarne, Antti. 1909. "Zum Märchen von der Tiersprache." *Zeitschrift des Vereins für Volkskunde* 19:299–303.

———. 1914. *Der Tiersprachenkundige Mann und Seine Neugierige Frau: Eine Vergleichende Märchenstudie.* FF Communications No. 15. Hamina: Suomalaisen Tiedeakatemian Kustantama.

Aicher, Georg. 1908. *Kamel und Nadelöhr. Eine kritisch-exegetische Studie über Mt. 19, 24 und Parallelen.* Münster: Verlag der Aschendorffschen Buchhandllung.

al-'Azm, Sadik Jalal. 1981. "Orientalism and Orientalism in Reverse." *Khamsin* 8:5–26.

al Faruqi, Lois Ibsen. 1987a. "The Cantillation of the *Qur'an*." *Asian Music* 19:2–25.

———. 1987b. "*Qur'an* Reciters in Competition in Kuala Lumpur." *Ethnomusicology* 31:221–28.

al Imam, Ahmad 'Ali. 1998. *Variant Readings of the Qur'an: A Critical Study of Their Historical and Linguistic Origins.* Herndon, Va.: The International Institute of Islamic Thought.

Aslam, Q. M. 1968. "Muhammad, A Psychological Essay." *Confinia Psychiatrica* 11:225–35.

Asmussen, Jes P. 1986. "'Kamel'—'Nadelöhr'." In *Studia Grammatica Iranica*, ed. Rüdiger Schmitt and Prods Oktor Skjaervo. 1–10. München: R. Kitzinger.

Baljon, J. M. S. 1961. *Modern Muslim Koran Interpretation (1880–1960).* Leiden: E. J. Brill.

Bateson, Mary Catherine. 1970. *Structural Continuity in Poetry: A Linguistic Study of Five Pre-Islamic Arabic Odes*. Paris: Mouton.

Bedford, Ian. 2001. "The Interdiction of Music in Islam." *The Australian Journal of Anthropology* 12:1–14.

Bellamy, James A. 1973. "The Mysterious Letters of the Koran: Old Abbreviations of the *Basmalah*." *Journal of the American Oriental Society* 93:267–85.

Benfey, Theodor. 1864. "Ein Märchen von der Tiersprache, Quelle und Verbreitung." *Orient und Occident* 2:133–71.

Benslama, Fethi. 1988. *La Nuit Brisée: Muhammad et l'énonciation islamique*. Paris: Éditions Ramsay.

Berg, Einar. 1966. "Muhammad: A Tentative Psychological Interpretation." *Temenos* 2:22–39.

Berkeley-Hill, Owen. 1921. "A Short Study of the Life and Character of Mohammed." *International Journal of Psycho-Analysis* 2:31–53.

Bødker, Laurits. 1965. *Folk Literature (Germanic)*. Copenhagen: Rosenkilde and Bagger.

Brandes, Stanley. 1985. *Forty: The Age and the Symbol*. Knoxville: University of Tennessee Press.

Brown, Norman O. 1983. "The Apocalypse of Islam." *Social Text* 3 (2):155–71.

Burton, John. 1972. "The Collection of the *Qur'an*." *Transactions of the Glasgow University Oriental Society* 23 (1969–1970):42–60.

———. 1977. *The Collection of the Qur'an*. Cambridge: Cambridge University Press.

———. 1988. "Linguistic Errors in the Qur'an." *Journal of Semitic Studies* 33:181–96.

Carlyle, Thomas. 1993. *On Heroes, Hero-Worship, and the Heroic in History*. Berkeley: University of California Press.

Cetin, Abdurrahman. 1999. "The Place of Music in Qur'anic Recitation." *American Journal of Islamic Social Sciences* 16:111–22.

Chaudhary, Muhammad A. 1995. "Orientalism on Variant Readings of the *Qur'an*: The Case of Arthur Jeffery." *The American Journal of Islamic Social Sciences* 12:170–84.

Chavannes, Édouard. 1910. *Cinq Cents Contes et Apologues: Extraits du Tripitaka Chinois*. Tome I. Paris: Ernest Leroux.

Chodkiewicz, Michel. 2001. "Les musulmans et la Parole de Dieu." *Revue de l'histoire des religions* 218:13–31.

Conrad, Lawrence I. 1987. "Abraha and Muhammad: Some Observations apropos of Chronology and Literary *Topoi* in the Early Arabic Historical Tradition." *Bulletin of the School of Oriental and African Studies* 50:225–40.

Cook, Michael. 2000. *The Qur'an: A Very Short Introduction*. Oxford: Oxford University Press.

Cowell, E. B., ed. 1895–1913. *The Jataka; or, Stories of the Buddha's Former Births*. 7 vols. Cambridge: Cambridge University Press.

Dashti, 'Ali. 1985. *Twenty Three Years: A Study of the Prophetic Career of Mohammad*. London: George Allen & Unwin.

Denny, Frederick M. 1980. "The *Adab* of Qur'an Recitation: Text and Context." In *International Congress for the Study of the* Qur'an, ed. A. H. Johns. 143–60. Canberra: Australian National University.

———. 1989. "*Qur'an* Recitation: A Tradition of Oral Performance and Transmission." *Oral Tradition* 4:5–26.

Dermenghem, Émile, Lounis Mahfoud, Suheyl Unver, and Nicolas de Witt. 1954–1961. "Les Sept Dormants d'Éphèse en Islam et en Chrétienté." *Revue des Études Islamiques* 22:59–112; 23:93–106; 25:1–11; 26:1–10; 27:1–8; 28:107–113; 29:1–18.

Donaldson, Bess Allen. 1937. "The Koran as Magic." *Moslem World* 27:254–66.

Donner, Fred M. 1998. *Narratives of Islamic Origins: The Beginnings of Islamic Historical Writing*. Princeton: The Darwin Press.

Doyle, Charles Clay. 1977. "Belaboring the Obvious: Sarcastic Interrogative Affirmatives and Negatives." *Maledicta* 1:77–82.

Duggan, Joseph J. 1966. "Formulas in the *Couronnement de Louis*." *Romania* 87:315–44.

———. 1973. *The Song of Roland: Formulaic Style and Poetic Craft*. Berkeley: University of California Press.

Dundes, Alan. 1967. "Some Minor Genres of American Folklore." *Southern Folklore Quarterly* 31:20–36.

———. 1999. *Holy Writ as Oral Lit: The Bible as Folklore*. Lanham, Md.: Rowman & Littlefield.

Elder, E. E. 1925. "Parallel Passages in the Koran (The Story of Moses)." *Moslem World* 15:254–59.

Farmer, Henry George. 1952. "The Religious Music of Islam." *Journal of the Royal Asiatic Society*, Parts 1 & 2:60–65.

Foley, John Miles. 1988. *The Theory of Oral Composition: History and Methodology*. Bloomington: Indiana University Press.

Frazer, James George. 1888. "The Language of Animals." *The Archaeological Review* 1:81–91; 161–81.

Freemon, Frank R. 1976. "A Differential Diagnosis of the Inspirational Spells of Muhammad the Prophet of Islam." *Epilepsia* 17:423–27.

Freud, Sigmund. 1955. *Moses and Monotheism*. New York: Vintage Books.

Glubb, John Bagot. 1979. *The Life and Times of Muhammad*. London: Hodder and Stoughton.

Gluck, J. J. 1982. "Is There Poetry in the *Qur'an*?" *Semitics* 8:43–89.

Graham, William A. 1987. *Beyond the Written Word: Oral Aspects of Scripture in the History of Religion*. Cambridge: Cambridge University Press.

———. 2001. "*Qur'an* as Spoken Word: An Islamic Contribution to the Understanding of Scripture." In *Approaches to Islam in Religious Studies*, ed. Richard C. Martin. 23–40. Oxford: Oneworld Publications.

Grey, Leslie. 1990. *A Concordance of Buddhist Birth Stories*. Oxford: The Pali Text Society.

Grimm, Jacob and Wilhelm. 1865. *Deutsche Sagen*. 2 vols. in one. Berlin: Nicolaische Verlagsbuchhandlung.

———. 1987. *The Complete Fairy Tales of the Brothers Grimm*. Trans. Jack Zipes. New York: Bantam.

Guidi, Ignazio. 1945. "Testi orientali inediti sopra I Sette Dormienti de Efeso." In *Raccolta di Scritti*. Vol. 1. 61–198. Roma: Istituto per l'Oriente.

Haase, Heinz-Wilhelm. 1966. Die Theodizeelegende vom Engel und dem Eremiten (AaTh 759). Ph.D. dissertation. Göttingen: Georg-August Universität.

Haddawy, Husain. 1990. *The Arabian Nights*. New York: W. W. Norton.

Haleem, Muhammad Abdel. 1992. "Grammatical Shift for Rhetorical Purposes: *Iltifat* and Related Features in the *Qur'an*." *Bulletin of the School of Oriental and African Studies* 55:407–32.

———. 2001. *Understanding the Qur'an: Themes and Style*. London: I. B. Tauris.

Hamès, Constant. 2001. "L'usage talismanique du Coran." *Revue de l'histoire des religions* 218:83–95.

Hartland, Edwin Sidney. 1890. *The Science of Fairy Tales*. London: Walter Scott.

Hasluck, F. W. 1912–1913. "The Forty." *Annual of the British School at Athens* 19:221–28.

Heller, Bernhard. 1904. "Éléments, Parallèles et Origine de la Légende des Sept Dormants." *Revue des Études Juives* 49:190–218.

Hirschkind, Charles. 1995. "Heresy or Hermeneutics: The Case of Nasr Hamid Abu Zayd." *Stanford Humanities Review* 5:35–48.

Hirt, Jean-Michel. 1993. *Le Miroir du Prophète: Psychanalyse et Islam*. Paris: Bernard Grasset.

Honigmann, Ernest. 1953. "Stephen of Ephesus and the Legend of the Seven Sleepers." In Ernest Honigmann, *Patristic Studies*. 125–68. Citta del Vaticano: Biblioteca Apostolica Vaticana.

Horodezky, S. A. 1913. "Der Zaddik." *Archiv für Religionswissenschaft* 16:145–59.

Huber, P. Michael. 1910. *Die Wanderlegende von den Siebenschläfern: Eine literargeschichtliche Untersuchung*. Leipzig: Otto Harrassowitz.

Ingham, Bruce. 1993. "The *Salfah* as a Narrative Genre." *Asian Folklore Studies* 52:5–32.

Izutsu, Toshihiko. 1964. *God and Man in the Koran: Semantics of the Koranic Weltanschauung*. Tokyo: The Keio Institute of Cultural and Linguistic Studies.

Jeffery, Arthur. 1938. *The Foreign Vocabulary of the Qur'an*. Baroda: Oriental Institute.

Jomier, Jacques. 1954. "Quelques positions actuelles de l'exégèse Coranique en Egypte: Révélées par une polemique récente (1941–1951)." *Mélanges Institut Dominicain d'Études Orientales du Caire*. 1:39–72.

Jones, Alan. 1994. Foreword and Introduction. *The Koran*. Trans. J. M. Rodwell. ix–xxvii. London: J. M. Dent.

———. 1996. "The Oral and the Written: Some Thoughts about the Quranic Text." In *Proceedings of the Colloquium on Logos, Ethos, Mythos in the Middle East & North Africa*, Part 1, ed. K. Dévényi and T. Iványi. 57–66. Budapest: Csoma de Körös Society.

Jourdan, François. 1983. *La tradition des sept dormants: une rencontre entre chrétiens et musulmans*. Paris: Editions Maisonneuve & Larose.

Juynboll, G. H. A. 1974. "The Position of *Qur'an* Recitation in Early Islam." *Journal of Semitic Studies* 19:240–51.

Kassis, Hanna E. 1983. *A Concordance of the Qur'an*. Berkeley: University of California Press.

Kellermann, Andreas. 1995. "Die 'Mündlichkeit' des Koran: Ein Forschungsgeschichtliches Problem der Arabistik." *Beiträge zur Geschichte der Sprachwissenschaft* 5:1–33.

Khalifa, Muhammad. 1983. *The Sublime Qur'an and Orientalism*. London: Longman.

Koch, John. 1883. *Die Siebenschläferlegende, ihr Ursprung und ihre Verbreitung: Eine mythologisch-literaturgeschicht-liche Studie*. Leipzig: Verlag von Carl Reissner.

König, Eduard. 1907. "Die Zahl vierzig und Verwandtes." *Zeitschrift der Deutschen Morgenländischen Gesellschaft* 61:913–17.

Kramer, Samuel Noah. 1959. *History Begins at Sumer*. Garden City: Doubleday Anchor Books.

Krauss, Friedrich S. 1908. "Vom wunderbaren Guslarengedächtnis." In *Slavische Volksforschungen: Abhandlungen über Glauben, Gewohnheitrechte, Sitten, Bräuche und die Guslarenlieder der Südslaven*. 183–89. Leipzig: Wilhelm Heims.

Krohn, Kaarle. 1971. *Folklore Methodology*. Austin: University of Texas Press.

Kurpershoek, P. Marcel. 1994. *Oral Poetry and Narratives from Central Arabia*. Vol. 1. Leiden: E. J. Brill.

Lee, Dorothy. 1950. "Codifications of Reality: Lineal and Nonlineal." *Psychosomatic Medicine* 12:89–97.

Lester, Toby. 1999. "What Is the Koran?" *The Atlantic Monthly* 283 (1):43–56.

Lévi, Israel. 1884. "La Légende de l'Ange et l'Ermite dans les Écrits Juifs." *Revue des Études Juives* 8:64–73, 202–5.

Lévy, Isidore. 1934. "Le chien des sept Dormants." In Joseph Bidez, *Mélanges Bidez*, 579–84. Bruxelles: Secretarat de L'Institut.

Lewis, Bernard. 1993. *Islam and the West*. Oxford: Oxford University Press.

Lichtenstein, Julius. 1959. "The Title of Voltaire's *Zadig*." *French Review* 33:65–67.

Lord, Albert. 1965. *The Singer of Tales*. New York: Atheneum.

———. 1986. "Perspectives on Recent Work on the Oral Traditional Formula." *Oral Tradition* 1:467–503.

Lüling, Günter. 1996. "Preconditions for the Scholarly Criticism of the Koran and Islam with Some Autobiographical Remarks." *The Journal of Higher Criticism* 3:73–109.

Lüthi, Max. 1976. *Once Upon a Time: On the Nature of Fairy Tales*. Bloomington: Indiana University Press.

McDonald, M. V. 1978. "Orally Transmitted Poetry in Pre-Islamic Arabic and Other Pre-literate Societies." *Journal of Arabic Literature* 9:14–31.

Mach, Rudolf. 1957. *Der Zaddik in Talmud und Midrash*. Leiden: E. J. Brill.

Magoun, Francis P., Jr. 1953. "The Oral-Formulaic Character of Anglo-Saxon Narrative Poetry." *Speculum* 28:446–67.

Manzoor, S. Parvez. 1986. "Islam and Orientalism: The Duplicity of a Scholarly Tradition." *Muslim World Book Review* 6:3–12.

———. 1987. "Method Against Truth: Orientalism and Qur'anic Studies." *Muslim World Book Review* 7:33–49.

Marzolph, Ulrich. 2000. "The Qoran and Jocular Literature." *Arabica* 47:478–87.

Massignon, Louis. 1969. *Opera Minora*. 3 vols. Paris: Presses Universitaires de France.

Minear, Paul S. 1942. "'The Needle's Eye.' A Study in Form Criticism." *Journal of Biblical Literature* 61:157–69.

Mir, Mustansir. 1989. *Verbal Idioms of the Qur'an*. Ann Arbor: Center for Near Eastern and North African Studies.

———. 1991. "Humor in the Qur'an." *The Muslim World* 81:179–93.

———. 1993. "The Sura as a Unity: A Twentieth Century Development in *Qur'an* Exegesis." In *Approaches to the Qur-an*, ed. G. R. Hawting and Abdul-Kader A. Shareef. 211–24. London: Routledge.

Monroe, James T. 1971. *Risalat at-Tawabi' Wa Z-Zawabi'. The Treatise of Familiar Spirits and Demons by Abut Amir ibn Shuhaid al-Ashja'i, al-Andalusi.* Berkeley: University of California Press.

———. 1972. "Oral Composition in Pre-Islamic Poetry." *Journal of Arabic Literature* 3:1–53.

———. 1997. "The Striptease That Was Blamed on Abu Bakr's Naughty Son: Was Father Being Shamed, or Was the Poet Having Fun? (Ibn Quzman's Zajal N. 133.)" In *Homoeroticism in Classical Arabic Literature*, ed. J. W. Wright, Jr., and Everett K. Rowson. 94–119. New York: Columbia University Press.

Motzki, Harald. 2001. "The Collection of the Qur'an: A Reconsideration of Western Views in Light of Recent Methodological Developments." *Der Islam* 78:1–34.

Moubarac, Youakim. 1961. "Le culte liturgique et populaire des Sept Dormants d'Ephèse (Ahl al-Kahf): trait d'union Orient-Occident entre l'Islam et La Chrétienté." *Studia Missionalia* 11:136–92.

Naddaff, Sandra. 1991. *Arabesque: Narrative Structure and the Aesthetics of Repetition in* 1001 Nights. Evanston: Northwestern University Press.

Nagel, Tilman. 1994. *"Qur'an." Enzyklopädie des Märchens* 8:274–81.

Nasr, Seyyed Hossein. 1972. *Ideals and Realities of Islam*. Boston: Beacon Press.

———. 1992. "Oral Transmission and the Book in Islamic Education: The Spoken and the Written Word." *Journal of Islamic Studies* 3:1–14.

Nelson, Christina. 1985. *The Art of Reciting the Quran*. Austin: University of Texas Press.

Nöldeke, Thedor. 1909. *Geschichte des Qorans*. Zweite Auflage. Leipzig: Dieterich'sche Verlagsbuchhandlung.

Noy, Dov. 1971. "The Jewish Versions of the 'Animal Languages' Folktale (AT 670): A Typological-Structural Study." In *Studies in Aggadah and Folk-Literature*, ed. Joseph Heinemann and Dov Noy. 171–208. Jerusalem: Magnes Press.

Oberhuber, Karl. 1985. "Nochmals 'Kamel' und Nadelöhr." In *Sprachwissenschaftliche Forschungen. Festschrift für Johann Knobloch*, ed. Hermann M. Olberg, Gernot Schmidt, and Heinz Bothien. 271–75. Innsbruck: Institut für Sprachwissenschaft der Universität Innsbruck.

Olrik, Axel. 1999. "Epic Laws of Folk Narrative." In *International Folkloristics*, ed. Alan Dundes. 83–97. Lanham, Md.: Rowman & Littlefield.

Paris, Gaston. 1881. "L'Ange et L'Ermite: Étude sur une Légende Religieuse." Académie des Inscriptions et Belles-Lettres, *Comptes Rendus des Seances de l'Année 1880* 8:427–49.

Parry, Adam, ed. 1971. *The Making of Homeric Verse: The Collected Papers of Milman Parry*. Oxford: Clarendon Press.

Pinker, Aron. 1994. "The Number 40 in the Bible." *Jewish Bible Quarterly* 22:163–72.

Puin, Gerd-R. 1996. "Observations on Early *Qur'an* Manuscripts in San'a." In *The Qur'an as Text*, ed. Stefan Wild. 107–11. Leiden: E. J. Brill.

Rahbar, Daud. 1963. "Aspects of the *Qur'an* Translation." *Babel* 9:60–68.

Rahman, Fazlur. 1980. *Major Themes of the Qur'an*. Minneapolis: Bibliotheca Islamica.

Rashid, Muhammad. 1995. "Was Muhammad Literate?" *Islamic Quarterly* 39:49–58.

Rasmussen, Anne K. 2001. "The Qur'an in Indonesian Daily Life: The Public Project of Musical Oratory." *Ethnomusicology* 45:30–57.

Rescher, Oskar. 1911. "Einiges über die Zahl Vierzig." *Zeitschrift der Deutschen Morgenländischen Gesellschaft* 65:517–20.

———. 1913. "Einige nachträgliche Bemerkungen zur Zahl 40 im Arabischen, Türkischen und Persischen." *Der Islam* 4:157–59.

Rippin, Andrew. 2000. "Muhammad in the *Qur'an*: Reading Scripture in the 21st Century." In *The Biography of Muhammad: The Issue of the Sources*, ed. Harald Motzki. 298–309. Leiden: E. J. Brill.

Roberts, Nancy N. 1993. "A Parable of Blessing: The Significance and Message of the Quranic Account of the Companions of the Cave." *Muslim World* 83:295–317.

Robinson, Neal. 1996. *Discovering the Qur'an: A Contemporary Approach to a Veiled Text*. London: SCM Press.

Robson, James. 1953. *An Introduction to the Science of Tradition*. London: The Royal Asiatic Society of Great Britain and Ireland.

———. 1957. "The Form of Muslim Tradition." *Transactions of the Glasgow University Oriental Society* (Years 1955 to 1956) 16:38–50.

Rodinson, Maxime. 1981. "A Critical Survey of Modern Studies on Muhammad." In *Studies on Islam*, ed. Merlin L. Swartz. 23–85. Oxford: Oxford University Press.

Róheim, Géza. 1953. "The Language of Birds." *American Imago* 10:3–14.

Roscher, Wilhelm Heinrich. 1909. "Die Zahl 40 im Glauben, Brauch und Schrifttum der Semiten." *Abhandlungen der Philologisch-Historischen Klasse der Königlich Sächsischen Gesellschaft der Wissenschaften* 27:91–138.

Rosenberg, Bruce A. 1970. *The Art of the American Folk Preacher*. New York: Oxford University Press.

Sabbagh, T. 1943. *La Métaphore dan le Coran*. Paris: Adrien-Maisonneuve.

Saeed, Abdullah. 1999. "Rethinking 'Revelation' as a Precondition for Reinterpreting the Qur'an: A Quranic Perspective." *Journal of Qur'anic Studies* 1:93–114.

Said, Edward W. 1978. *Orientalism*. New York: Pantheon Books.

al-Said, Labib. 1975. *The Recited Koran: A History of the First Recorded Version*. Princeton: The Darwin Press.

Sartori, Paul. 1935–1936. Siebenschläfer. *Handwörterbuch des deutschen Aberglaubens*. Band VII. Pp. 1702–4. Berlin: Walter de Gruyter.

Schönbach, Anton E. 1901. *Die Legende vom Engel und Waldbruder*. Wien: K. Gerold's Sohn.

Schwarzbaum, Haim. 1959. "Jewish and Moslem Versions of Some Theodicy Legends." *Fabula* 3:119–69.

———. 1982. *Biblical and Extra-Biblical Legends in Islamic Folk-Literature*. Walldorf-Hessen: Verlag für Orientkunde.

Sells, Michael. 1999. *Approaching the Qur'an: The Early Revelations*. Ashland, Ore.: White Cloud Press.

Serrano, Richard. 2002. *Neither a Borrower: Forging Traditions in French, Chinese and Arabic Poetry*. Oxford: Legenda.

Sfeir, George N. 1998. "Basic Freedoms in a Fractured Legal Culture: Egypt and the Case of Nasr Hamid Abu Zayd." *Middle East Journal* 52:402–14.

Shakir, Muhammad. 1926. "On the Translation of the *Qur'an* into Foreign Languages." *Muslim World* 16:161–65.

Sidersky, D. 1933. *Les Origines des Légendes Musulmanes dans Le Coran et dans les Vies des Prophètes.* Paris: Librairie Orientaliste Paul Geuthner.

Sowayan, Saad Abdullah. 1985. *Nabati Poetry: The Oral Poetry of Arabia.* Berkeley: University of California Press.

———. 1992. *The Arabian Oral Historical Narrative: An Ethnographic and Linguistic Analysis.* Wiesbaden: Otto Harrassowitz.

Speight, R. Marston. 1989. "Oral Traditions of the Prophet Muhammad: A Formulaic Approach." *Oral Tradition* 4:27–37.

Sprenger, Aloys. 1889. *Mohammed und der Koran. Eine psychologische Studie.* Hamburg: J. F. Richter.

Stephan, Stephan H. 1928. "Studies in Palestinian Folklore and Custom: The Number Forty." *Journal of the Palestine Oriental Society* 8:214–22.

Stetkevych, Suzanne Pinckney. 1997. "Intoxication and Immortality: Wine and Associated Imagery in al-Ma'arri's Garden." In *Homoeroticism in Classical Arabic Literature,* ed. J. W. Wright, Jr., and Everett K. Rowson, 210–32. New York: Columbia University Press

Talbi, Muhammad. 1958. "La Qira'a bi-l-alhan." *Arabica* 5:183–90.

Taylor, Archer. 1949. "Locutions for 'Never.'" *Romance Philology* 2:103–34.

Thompson, Stith. 1955–1958. *Motif-Index of Folk-Literature.* 6 vols. 2d ed. Bloomington: Indiana University Press.

Tibawi, A. L. 1979. "Second Critique of English-Speaking Orientalists and Their Approach to Islam and the Arabs." *Islamic Quarterly* 23:3–47.

Touma, Habib Hassan. 1975. "Die *Qur'an*rezitation: Eine Form der Religiosen Musik der Araber." *Baessler-Archiv* 23:87–133.

Tritton, A. S. 1971. "The Camel and the Needle's Eye." *Bulletin of the School of Oriental and African Studies* 34:139.

van Gennep, Arnold. 1909. *La Question d'Homère: Les Poemes homèriques, l'archéologie et la poésie populaire.* Paris: Mercure de France.

Waardenburg, Jean-Jacques. 1962. *L'Islam dans le Miroir de l'Occident.* The Hague: Mouton.

Wansbrough, John. 1977. *Quranic Studies*. Oxford: Oxford University Press.

Warraq, Ibn. 1995. *Why I Am Not a Muslim*. Amherst, N.Y.: Prometheus Books.

———. 1998. *The Origins of the Qur'an: Classic Essays on Islam's Holy Book*. Amherst, N.Y.: Prometheus Books.

———. 2000. *The Quest for the Historical Muhammad*. Amherst, N.Y.: Prometheus Books.

Watt, W. Montgomery. 1955. "Carlyle on Muhammad." *The Hibbert Journal* 53:247–54.

———. 1970. *Bell's Introduction to the Qur'an*. Edinburgh: Edinburgh University Press.

———. 1972. "The Camel and the Needle's Eye." *Studies in the History of Religions* 22:155–58.

Welch, Alford T. 2000. "Formulaic Features of the Punishment-Stories." In *Literary Structures of Religious Meaning in the Qur'an*, ed. Issa J. Boullata. 77–116. Richmond: Curzon.

Weyh, Wilhelm. 1911. "Zur Geschichte der Siebenschläfer-legende." *Zeitschrift der Deutschen Morgenländischen Gesellschaft* 65:289–301.

Wheeler, Brannon M. 1998. "The Jewish Origins of *Qur'an* 18:65–82? Reexamining Arent Jan Wensinck's Theory." *Journal of the American Oriental Society* 118:153–71.

Wild, Stefan. 1993. "Die andere seite des textes: Nasr Hamid Abu Zaid und der Koran." *Die Welt des Islams* 33:256–61.

———, ed. 1996. *The Qur'an as Text*. Leiden: E. J. Brill.

Zakaria, Rafiq. 1991. *Muhammad and the Quran*. London: Penguin.

Zeid, Nasr Abou. 1999. *Critique du discours religieux*. Arles: Actes Sud-Sindbad.

Zwemer, Samuel M. 1939. *Studies in Popular Islam*. London: The Sheldon Press.

Zwettler, Michael J. 1976. "Classical Arabic Poetry between Folk and Oral Tradition." *Journal of the American Oriental Society* 96:198–212.

———. 1978. *The Oral Tradition of Classical Arabic Poetry: Its Character and Implications*. Columbus: Ohio State University Press.

Index

Aarne, Antti, 54, 63
Aarne-Thompson tale types, 54, 60, 62, 64, 65
Abdollah, 31
Abraham, 30, 66
abrogation, 7, 33
Abu Zayd, Nasr Hamid, 11–12, 22
Achilles, 30
Allah, 2, 3, 5, 7, 8, 11, 24, 25, 27; attitudes towards unbelievers, 36–39; attributes of, 31; powers of, 32–35, 56–57; rules for the faithful, 40–53; utilization of folklore by, 66, 67, 70, 71
alms, 39–40
Amina, 6
Anderson, Walter, 4
"The Animal Languages" (tale type), 62–64
ant, 25, 62–64
Arabian Nights, 53, 64
Arberry, A. J., 24
Ayesha, 6

Barbarossa, 61
Bateson, Gregory, 18
Bateson, Mary Katherine, 18
bismallah, 50, 51
book, *Qur'an* perceived as, 14, 30
Brown, Norman O., 61

Cairo, 22
Carlyle, Thomas, ix, xi
Christians, 10, 20, 25, 30, 36, 40, 56, 61, 65
"Cinderella" (tale type), 54
concordance, value of, xiii, 24, 70
contradictions, 7–8

Daniel, 1
David, 30
Day of Judgment, 3, 25, 26, 40–41, 42, 56, 70
Day of Resurrection, 40
"Debate of the Belly and the Members" (tale type), 67
dog, 55, 59, 70
Duggan, Joseph, 18
duplicate passages, 26–29

Ecclesiastes, 49
Eos, 30

epic laws. *See* law of repetition; law of single-strandedness
epithets, particularistic versus generic, 30

fables of the ancients, 53–54, 67–68, 71
fixed phrase folklore genres, 19
Foley, John Miles, 16
folklore, 12, 68; characteristics of, 47
folktales in the *Qur'an*, 54–64
food taboos, 41
formula, definition of, 16–17; in Homeric epics, 30; surviving translation, 24
formulaic density, 17–18, 65
forty, 3, 62; as ritual number, 65–66
Freud, Sigmund, 14

Gabriel, 1, 2, 5, 6, 9, 14, 65, 66
"Gardens of Eden," 44
Gehenna, 25, 29, 45
genies. See *jinn*
"God's Justice Vindicated" (The Angel and the Hermit) (tale type), 60
Grimm brothers, 58

hadith, 6
Heaven, 44
Hejaiej, Monia, x
Hell, 45
Hera, 30
historicity, 6, 20, 28
Homer, 15, 17, 19, 30
houris, 8, 44

Husain, Taha, 12

Iblis, 35. *See also* Satan
illiterate, Muhammad said to be, 2
inerrancy, 5
Ingham, Bruce, 69
inimitability of *Qur'an*, 4–5
Islam, ix, 1, 5, 10, 13, 21; principles of, 39–40, 42
isnad, 5

Jataka tale, 63
Jerusalem, 6
Jesus, 1, 10, 38, 66, 79
Jewish tradition, 20, 21, 61, 63, 65
Jews, 25, 30, 36, 40
jinn, 11–12, 19, 62
John the Baptist, 1
Joseph, 30, 66
Judgment Day. *See* Day of Judgment
"Judgment of Solomon" (tale type), 67

Kassis, Hanna E., xiii, 24, 70
Khadija, 6
Khalafallah, Mohammad Ahmad, 12–13
Krauss, Friedrich, 16–17
Kurpershoek, P. Marcel, 68
Kyffhuser, 62

language of the birds. *See* "The Animal Languages" (tale type)
law of repetition, 53
"Law of Self Correction," 4
law of single-strandedness, 66
Lebanon, 21

Index 87

legend versus folktale, 58, 62
Leviticus, 41
Lewis, Bernard, 20
linear worldview, 66
linguistic errors, 5
"Little Red Riding Hood" (tale type), 54
locutions for *never*, 38
Lord, Albert, 16
Lot, 30
Lüling, Günter, 13

Massignon, Louis, 61
Mead, Margaret, 18
Mecca, 3, 6
Medina, 3
"Messenger of Allah" (epithet), 36
metahistory, 66
migratory legend, 58
Monroe, James T., xiii, 19
Moses, 10, 28, 29, 59, 66
Moses and Monotheism, 14
Motif-Index of Folk-Literature, 56, 62
Muhammad, ix, 1, 2, 3, 4, 5, 6, 7, 13, 14, 19, 31, 36, 41, 45, 53, 54, 55, 65, 66, 67; illiterate, said to be, 2
multiple existence, characteristic of folklore, 47
musical, term not used in reference to Qur'anic recitation, 21–22

Nasr, Seyyed Hossein, 69
New Testament, x, 1, 25, 27, 29, 49, 66, 67
night journey, 6
Noah, 29, 36

Noldeke, Theodor, 3, 20
numerical variation, 28

Odysseus, 30
Oedipal configuration, 6–7, 14
Old Testament, x, 27, 29, 30, 36, 49, 66, 67
Olrik Axel, 53, 66
opening formulas, 55
oral-formulaic theory, 15–20
oral formulas in the *Qur'an*, 23–54
oral literary coda, 51
oral transmission of the *Qur'an*, 14–15, 23, 27, 65
Orientalism, 10, 20–21, 65, 68

parable, 1, 57, 70
Paradise, 8, 38, 44
Parry, Milman, 16, 30
People of the Book, 36
Pharaoh, 28, 29
pointed rhetorical question, 39
Potiphar's Wife motif, 66
pronominal flexibility, 45–47
proverb, 49
Psalms, 57
push-button telephone, 50

quarantine, 65
Queen of Sheba, 50
Qur'an, ix, x, xi, xiii, 1–15, 19, 20, 21, 22; folkloristic aspects of, 65, 66, 67, 68, 69, 70, 71; folktales in, 54–64; formulas in, 23–54

Ramadan, 3
recitation of *Qur'an* competitions, 15

reluctance to consider the *Qur'an* from a folkloristic perspective, explanation of, 20, 22
repetition, law of, 53
Resurrection, belief in, 56. *See also* Day of Resurrection
revelation, issue of, 67
Robson, James, 23

Said, Edward, 20
salfih, 68
Satan, attributes of, 22, 35–36; not to be trusted, 42
scales of justice, 25
Schwarzbaum, Haim, 60, 61
"The Seven Sleepers" (tale type), 55–59
single-strandedness, law of, 66
Solomon, 30, 50, 62, 63
Sowayan, Saad, 18, 68–69
surah, definition of, 3

Tehran, 50
Ten Commandments, 43
Thompson, Stith, 54, 56, 61
"Thou Shalt Not Kill," 43
tongue of truth, 24

Torah, 1, 30
translations of *Qur'an*, mistrust of, 9–10
triad of sins, 8

unbelievers, 25, 27, 36–39, 49, 52, 53, 56, 67, 70, 71
Uthman, Caliph, 4

van Gennep, Arnold, 17
variation, characteristic of folklore, 47
Verzeichnis der Märchentypen, 54
Virgin Mary, 1
Voltaire, 60

weather, 34
wine, prohibition against, 8
word of God, 5, 9, 27, 67, 69

years thought days (motif), 57
Yemen, 4

Zacharias, 1
Zaddik, 61
Zadig, 60–61
Zaynab, 6, 7

About the Author

Alan Dundes is professor of anthropology and folklore at the University of California, Berkeley, and a leading authority in the study of folklore. He is the author or editor of more than thirty books including *Two Tales of Crow and Sparrow: A Freudian Folkloristic Essay on Caste and Untouchability*, *Holy Writ as Oral Lit: The Bible as Folklore*, and *International Folkloristics*.